501 GRAMMAR & WRITING QUESTIONS

501 GRAMMAR & WRITING QUESTIONS
2nd Edition

LEARNINGEXPRESS

New York

Library of Congress Catalonging-in-Publication Data:
501 grammar & writing questions.—2nd ed.
    p. cm.
  ISBN 1-57685-400-0
  1. English language—Grammar—Examinations, questions, etc. 2. English
language—Rhetoric—Examinations, questions, etc. 3. Report writing—
Examinations, questions, etc. I. Title: 501 grammar and writing questions.
II. Title: Five hundred one grammar and writing questions. III. Title: Five
hundred and one grammar and writing questions.

PE1112 .A15 2002
428.2'076—dc21

              2001038996

Printed in the United States of America
9 8 7 6 5 4 3 2 1
Second Edition

ISBN 1-57685-400-0

For more information or to place an order, contact LearningExpress at:
    900 Broadway
    Suite 604
    New York, NY 10003

Or Visit us at:
    www.learnatest.com

CONTENTS

501 GRAMMAR & WRITING QUESTIONS

INTRODUCTION

This book—which can be used alone, along with another writing-skills text of your choice, or in combination with the LearningExpress publication, *Writing Skills Success in 20 Minutes a Day*—will give you practice dealing with capitalization, punctuation, basic grammar, sentence structure, organization, paragraph development, and essay writing. It is designed to be used by individuals working on their own and for teachers or tutors helping students to learn or review basic writing skills. Practice with *501 Grammar and Writing Questions* should go a long way in alleviating writing anxiety, too!

Many people grimace when faced with grammar exercises. But in order to communicate with others, pass tests, and get your point across in writing, using words and punctuation effectively is a necessary skill. Maybe you're one of the millions of people who, as a student in elementary or high school, found memorizing grammar rules tedious. Maybe you were confused by all of the *exceptions* to those rules. Maybe, you thought they would just come naturally as you continued to write and speak.

First, know you are not alone. It is true that some people work very hard to understand the rules, while others seem to have a natural gift for writing. And that's okay; we all have unique talents. Still, it's a fact that on most jobs today, good communication skills—including writing—are essential. The good news is that grammar and writing skills can be developed with practice.

Learn by doing. It's an old lesson, tried and true. And it's the tool this book is designed to give you. The 501 grammar and writing questions in this book will provide you with lots of practice. As you work through each set of questions, you'll be gaining a solid understanding of basic grammar and usage rules. And all without memorizing! The purpose of this book is to help you improve your language skills through encouragement, not frustration.

AN OVERVIEW

501 Grammar and Writing Questions is divided into six sections:

Section 1: Mechanics: Capitalization and
         Punctuation
Section 2: Sentence Structure
Section 3: Agreement
Section 4: Modifiers
Section 5: Paragraph Development
Section 6: Essay Questions

Each section is subdivided into short sets of between eight and twenty questions each. The book is specifically organized to help you build confidence as you further develop your written-language skills. *501 Grammar and Writing Questions* begins with the basic mechanics of capitalization and punctuation, and then moves on to grammar and sentence structure. By the time you reach the section on paragraph development, you've already practiced on almost 300 questions. In Section 5, you continue practicing the skills you've already begun to master in the previous four sections, this time in combination. When you get to the last section, you'll be ready to write your own essays.

HOW TO USE THIS BOOK

Whether you're working alone or helping someone brush up on grammar and usage, this book will give you the opportunity to practice, practice, practice.

WORKING ON YOUR OWN

If you are working alone to review the basics or prepare for a test in connection with a job or school, you will probably want to use this book in combination with a basic grammar and usage text, or with *Writing Skills Success in 20 Minutes a Day*. If you're fairly sure of your basic language-mechanics skills, however, you can use *501 Grammar and Writing Questions* by itself.

Use the answer key at the end of the book not only to find out if you got the right answer, but also to learn how to tackle similar kinds of questions next time. Every answer is explained. Make sure you understand the explanations—usually by going back to the questions—before moving on to the next set.

TUTORING OTHERS

This book will work well in combination with almost any basic grammar and usage text. You will probably find it most helpful to give students a brief lesson in the particular operation they'll be learning—capitalization, punctuation, subject-verb agreement, pronoun agreement, sentence structure, style—and then have them spend the remainder of the session actually answering the questions in the sets. You will want to impress upon them the importance of learning by doing, checking their answers, and reading the explanations carefully. Make sure they understand a particular set of questions before you assign the next one.

ADDITIONAL RESOURCES

For more detailed explanations of English grammar and usage rules, you may want to buy—or borrow from the library—one or more of the following books:

Eggenschwiller, Jean and Emily Dotson Biggs. *Cliff's Quick Review Writing: Grammar, Usage, and Style* (New York: Hungry Minds, Inc., 2001).

Feierman, Joanne. *Actiongrammar: Fast, No-Hassle Answers on Everyday Usage and Punctuation* (New York: Fireside, 2001).

Goddin, Nell and Erik Palma. *Grammar Smart: A Guide to Perfect Usage* (New York: Villard Books, 1993).

Hollander, Joseph. *21st Century Grammar Handbook* (New York: Dell Books, 1993).

Lerner, Marcia. *Writing Smart: Your Guide to Great Writing* (New York: Villard Books, 1993).

Olson, Judith F. *Writing Skills Success in 20 Minutes a Day* (New York: LearningExpress, 1998).

O'Conner, Patricia T. *Woe Is I: The Grammarphobe's Guide to Better English in Plain English* (New York: Riverhead Books, 1998).

Straus, Jane. *The Blue Book of Grammar and Punctuation* (Mill Valley, CA: Bare Bones Training & Consulting Company, 2001).

Swan, Michael. *Practical English Usage* (New York: Oxford University Press, 1995).

The American Heritage Book of English Usage: A Practical and Authoritative Guide to Contemporary English (Boston: Houghton Mifflin, 1996).

S·E·C·T·I·O·N 1

MECHANICS: CAPITALIZATION AND PUNCTUATION

Since every sentence begins with a capital, the how-to's of capitalization seem like a logical place to begin learning about language mechanics. When doing the exercises in this section, refer to the checklist below. Matching your answer to a rule will reinforce the mechanics of writing and secure that knowledge for you.

CAPITALIZATION CHECKLIST

✓ The first word of every sentence→*Yes, we do carry the matching bed skirt.*

✓ The first word of a quoted sentence (not just a quoted phrase)→*And with great flourish, he sang, "O beautiful for gracious skies, for amber waves of grain!"*

✓ The specific name of a person (and his or her title), a place, or a thing (otherwise known as *proper nouns*). *Proper nouns* include specific locations and geographic regions, political, social and athletic organizations and agencies, historical events, documents and periods, nationalities and their language, religions, their members and their deities, brand or trade names, and holidays.

✓ The abbreviation for *proper nouns*. Government agencies are probably the most frequently abbreviated. Remember to capitalize each letter.→*The* CIA *makes me feel very secure.*

✓ Adjectives (descriptive words) derived from *proper nouns*. Ex: *America (proper noun)*→the *American (adjective) flag*

✓ The *pronoun* "I".

✓ The most important words in a title→Last *March, I endured a twenty-hour public reading of Moby Dick.*

PUNCTUATION CHECKLIST

PERIODS

✓ At the end of a declarative sentence (sentence that makes a statement)→*Today, I took a walk to nowhere.*

✓ At the end of a command or request→ *Here's a cloth. Now gently burp the baby on your shoulder.*

✓ At the end of an indirect question→*Jane asked if I knew where she had left her keys.*

✓ Before a decimal number→*Statisticians claim that the average family raises 2.5 children.*

✓ Between dollars and cents→*I remember when a $1.50 could buy the coolest stuff.*

✓ After an initial in a person's name→*You are Sir James W. Dewault, are you not?*

✓ After an abbreviation→*On Jan. 12, I leave for Africa.*

QUESTION MARKS

✓ At the end of a question→*Why do you look so sad?*

✓ Inside a quotation mark when the quote is a question→*She asked, "Why do you look so sad?"*

EXCLAMATION POINTS

✓ At the end of a word, phrase, or sentence filled with emotion→*Oh my God! There are the Backstreet Boys!*

✓ Inside a quotation mark when the quote is an exclamation→*The teenage girl screamed, "Oh my God! There are the Backstreet Boys!"*

QUOTATION MARKS

✓ When directly quoting dialogue, not when paraphrasing→*Hamlet says, "To be, or not to be. That is the question."*

✓ For titles of chapters, articles, short stories, poems, songs, or periodicals→*My favorite short story is "Flowers for Algernon."*

SEMICOLONS

✓ Between two independent clauses (An independent clause is a complete thought. It has a subject and a predicate.)→*Edward joined the basketball team; remarkably, the 5′4″ young man excelled at the sport.*

✓ Between elements in a series that uses commas→*The possible dates for the potluck dinner are Thursday, June 5; Saturday, June 7; or Monday, June 9.*

COLONS

✓ Between two complete ideas when the second idea explains the first.→*Keri pushed her dinner away: She had eaten on the car ride home.*

✓ Before a list→*Grandma brought Charlize's favorite three sweets: caramel candies, Sugar Daddies, and Charm's Blow Pops.*

✓ Between titles and subtitles→*Measurement: Translating into Metric*

✓ Between volumes and page numbers→*Marvel Comics 21:24*

✓ Between chapters and verse→*Job 4:12*

✓ Between hours and minutes→*It's 2:00 A.M.—time to sleep.*

APOSTROPHES

✓ Where letters or numbers have been deleted—as in a contraction→*I looked at my father and whispered, "It's (It is) okay to cry every so often."*

✓ At the end of a name where there is ownership. (Remember to also add an *s* after the apostrophe if the word or name does not end in an *s* already)→*Mary Jane's horse sprained his ankle during practice.*

COMMAS

✓ Between items in dates and addresses→*Michael arrived at Ellis Island, New York, on February 14, 1924.*

✓ Between words in a list→*The university hired a woman to direct the Bursar's, Financial Aid, and Registrar's offices.*

✓ Between equally important adjectives (Be careful not to separate adjectives that describe each other)→*The reporter spoke with several intense, talented high school athletes.*

✓ After a tag that precedes a direct quote→*David whined, "I am famished."*

✓ In a quote that precedes a tag and is not a question or an exclamation→*"I am famished," whined David.*

✓ Around non-essential clauses, parenthetical phrases, and appositives (A non-essential or non-restrictive clause is a word or group of words that are not necessary for the sentence's completion; a parenthetical phrase interrupts the flow of a sentence; and an appositive is a word or group of words that rename the noun preceding them)→*Matt's mother, Janie* (appositive),*who has trouble with directions*(non-essential clause), *had to ask for help.*

✓ After introductory words, phrases, and clauses→*Hoping for the best, we checked our luggage.*

✓ Before conjunctions (Conjunctions are words that link two independent clauses together)→*Drew wanted to experience ballroom dancing before his wedding, so he signed up for lessons at a local hall.*

SET 1 (Answers begin on page 119.)

For the following questions, choose the lettered part of the sentence that contains a word that needs a capital letter. If no additional words should be capitalized, choose answer **e**. Refer to the checklist at the beginning of the chapter if you want to be certain about your answer.

1. My physician, | dr. Holly Watts, told me that | I was healthy enough | to run in the Boston marathon. |

   a   b   c   d

   None

   e

2. At the party, | the hostess served | pastries | and irish coffee. | None

   a   b   c   d   e

3. Alan Farnham, jr., was so lazy | that no one wanted to | be on the committee | with him. | None

   a   b   c   d   e

4. Doug shouted angrily, | "why am I the one | who always has to | do the dishes?" | None

   a   b   c   d   e

5. The Constitution of | the United States certainly | cannot be considered | an ordinary constitution. |

   a   b   c   d

   None

   e

6. Tommy's Bar and grill was | conveniently located on | one of the main streets |

   a   b   c

   in downtown Waynesberg. | None

   d   e

7. My peach-colored dog, | whose name is penny, | is a fine example of |

   a   b   c

   an intelligent, brave, and loyal toy poodle. | None

   d   e

8. Her name used to be Heather, | but she changed it | after the movie heathers |

   a   b   c

   came out a few years ago. | None.

   d   e

SET 2 (Answers begin on page 119.)
Choose the punctuation mark that is needed in each of the following sentences. If no additional punctuation is needed, choose answer **e**.

9. "I can't believe it!" shouted Karen. My blue socks have holes in them!"
    a. .
    b. ,
    c. !
    d. "
    e. none

10. My three cats, Shadow, Dave, and Roy like liver-flavored kitty treats best.
    a. ;
    b. —
    c. !
    d. ,
    e. none

11. The following are my favorite foods biscuits, gravy, mashed potatoes, and French-cut green beans.
    a. :
    b. ,
    c. .
    d. ;
    e. none

12. Max was so angry he stalked out fifteen minutes later he came back.
    a. ;
    b. ,
    c. ?
    d. :
    e. none

13. We were all surprised when Mayor Bonita Perez—a petite, conservatively dressed woman threw a perfect pitch to the catcher at the opening of the first game of the season.
    a. ;
    b. ,
    c. —
    d. :
    e. none

14. Jacks hair, usually so neatly combed, is a mess today, as if he slept on it strangely.
    a. '
    b. ,
    c. ;
    d. .
    e. none

15. After his vacation in the Rockies, Ramon decided to give up mountain-climbing for good.
    a. ,
    b. ;
    c. —
    d. .
    e. none

16. "I wonder" Syad mused, "if he knew what he did was wrong."
    a. ?
    b. ,
    c. :
    d. ;
    e. none

17. Big Bob Bailey our basketball coach, is the toughest man alive.
   a. :
   b. ;
   c. —
   d. ,
   e. none

18. My favorite books are ones about baseball it's my favorite sport.
   a. ,
   b. ?
   c. ;
   d. !
   e. none

SET 3 (Answers begin on page 120.)
Choose the answer that shows the best punctuation for the underlined part of the sentence. If the sentence is correct as is, choose **e**.

19. Cats make wonderful <u>pets even though they</u> seem closer to being wild than dogs are.
   a. pets, even though, they
   b. pets, even though they
   c. pets. Even though they
   d. pets; even though they
   e. correct as is

20. Many people believe in <u>UFO's however I've</u> never seen one.
   a. UFO's however: I've
   b. UFO's, however, I've
   c. UFO's however, I've
   d. UFO's; however, I've
   e. correct as it is

21. "Am I <u>crazy," asked Samantha, "Am</u> I the only one who thinks volleyball is a waste of time?"
   a. crazy?" asked Samatha. "Am
   b. crazy?" asked Samatha, "Am
   c. crazy," asked Samatha? "Am
   d. crazy?" asked Samatha, "Am
   e. correct as it is

22. Some scientists <u>maintain that we</u> are born with a fear of snakes.
   a. maintain, that we
   b. maintain that, we
   c. maintain: that we
   d. maintain—that we
   e. correct as it is

23. After the dog frightened the mail <u>carrier, the dogs</u> owner apologized over and over.
   a. carrier the dogs
   b. carrier, the dog's
   c. carrier, the dogs'
   d. carrier the dogs'
   e. correct as is

24. The <u>people who are at the back of the line</u> should move to the front.
   a. people, who are at the back of the line
   b. people who are at the back of the line,
   c. people, who are at the back of the line,
   d. people who, are at the back of the line,
   e. correct as is

25. The students asked whether I thought there would be a woman <u>president within the next decade?</u>
   a. president within the next decade!
   b. president, within the next decade.
   c. president within the next decade.
   d. president, within the next decade?
   e. correct as is

26. This is the first time you have ever been to a major league baseball <u>game, isn't it?</u>
  a. game isn't it?
  b. game, is'nt it?
  c. game, isn't it.
  d. game isn't it.
  e. correct as is

27. Chicken <u>pox a virus</u> is very contagious.
  a. pox, a virus,
  b. pox, a virus
  c. pox, a virus—
  d. pox a virus,
  e. correct as is

28. I was born on <u>May 17, 1962 in Corvallis, Oregon.</u>
  a. May 17 1962 in Corvallis, Oregon.
  b. May 17 1962, in Corvallis Oregon.
  c. May 17, 1962 in Corvallis, Oregon.
  d. May 17, 1962, in Corvallis, Oregon.
  e. correct as is

SET 4 (Answers begin on page 120.)
For each question, find the sentence that has a mistake in capitalization or punctuation. If you find no mistakes, mark choice **d**.

29. a. My favorite season is Spring.
  b. Last Monday, Aunt Ruth took me shopping.
  c. We elected Ben as treasurer of the freshman class.
  d. No mistakes.

30. a. My best friend is moving to another city.
  b. "What time does the movie begin?" he asked.
  c. The boys' wore identical sweaters.
  d. No mistakes.

31. a. She asked me, to show her how to make an apple pie.
  b. He shouted from the window, but we couldn't hear him.
  c. Occasionally, someone will stop and ask for directions.
  d. No mistakes.

32. a. Science and math are my two best subjects.
  b. We met senator Moynihan at a conference last June.
  c. Did you see the movie Babe?
  d. No mistakes.

33. a. When you come to the end of Newton Road, turn left onto Wilson Blvd.
  b. A small river runs alongside the highway.
  c. We learned that cape Cod was formed 20,000 years ago.
  d. No mistakes.

34. a. The tour guide asked us if we had any questions?
  b. Lauren's father is an auto mechanic.
  c. We asked if he could give us change for a dollar.
  d. No mistakes.

35. a. Did you read that article in Newsweek?
  b. My Uncle took us to Yankee Stadium.
  c. Christina has a Persian cat named Snowball.
  d. No mistakes.

36. a. "I'll come and stay with you, grandma," I said.
  b. "Don't ever tell a lie," he warned.
  c. "Why won't you play with us?" he asked.
  d. No mistakes.

37.
  a. I always have a hard time getting up in the morning.
  b. We took: a tent, a cooler, and a sleeping bag.
  c. The fog was as thick as potato soup.
  d. No mistakes.

38.
  a. This is someone elses coat.
  b. Which of these songs was recorded by Bruce Springsteen?
  c. That book must be yours.
  d. No mistakes.

39.
  a. Don't stand in my way.
  b. Cecilia and I fought our way through the crowd.
  c. The vegetables were old rubbery and tasteless.
  d. No mistakes.

40.
  a. Remember to walk the dog.
  b. "Don't run"! Mr. Ellington shouted.
  c. It's supposed to snow today and tomorrow.
  d. No mistakes.

41.
  a. Charleen's parents worried whenever she drove the car.
  b. Who designed the Brooklyn Bridge?
  c. Diseases like Smallpox and Polio have been eradicated.
  d. No mistakes.

42.
  a. Can you find the Indian ocean on this map?
  b. Which river, the Nile or the Amazon, is longer?
  c. Lerner Avenue runs into the Thompson Parkway.
  d. No mistakes.

43.
  a. He's the best dancer in the school.
  b. We were planning to go, but the meeting was canceled.
  c. "Okay," she said, I'll go with you."
  d. No mistakes.

44.
  a. Does Judge Parker live on your street?
  b. Twenty government officials met to deal with Wednesday's crisis.
  c. The Mayor spoke at a news conference this morning.
  d. No mistakes.

45.
  a. My brother, Isaac, is the best player on the team.
  b. Because of the high cost; we decided not to go.
  c. Where's your new puppy?
  d. No mistakes.

46.
  a. I have learned to appreciate Mozart's music.
  b. My cousin Veronica is studying to be a Veterinarian.
  c. Mr. Shanahan is taller than Professor Martin.
  d. No mistakes.

47.
  a. "You look just like your mother," Ms. Jones told me.
  b. "Please be careful," he said.
  c. Tyler asked, "why do I have to go to bed so early?"
  d. No mistakes.

48.
  a. Do you prefer root beer or orange soda?
  b. In which year did world war II end?
  c. I like to study the geography of the Everglades.
  d. No mistakes.

49. a. Colds like many other viruses are highly contagious.
    b. Call me when you feel better.
    c. Did you wash your hands, Michael?
    d. No mistakes.

50. a. The industrial revolution began in Europe.
    b. Is Labor Day a national holiday?
    c. General Patton was a four-star general.
    d. No mistakes.

51. a. Carmen brought bread, and butter, and strawberry jam.
    b. Let's look at the map.
    c. Be sure to thank Aunt Helen for the gift.
    d. No mistakes.

52. a. My Aunt Georgia loves to read Eighteenth-Century novels.
    b. Eli's sister's cousin lives in Alaska.
    c. Is that a German shepherd?
    d. No mistakes.

53. a. Those shoes are too expensive.
    b. Michael's best friend is Patrick.
    c. Did you hear that Inez got a new puppy.
    d. No mistakes.

SET 5 (Answers begin on page 121.)
Questions 54–57 are based on the following passage. First read the passage, and then choose the answer that shows the best capitalization and punctuation for each underlined part.

Madam Helena P. 54) <u>Blavatsky born</u> in Russia on May 8, 1831, claimed to have psychic powers and to be capable of performing feats of clairvoyance and telepathy. During her sixty years, she traveled to many 55) <u>countries—including</u> the United States, England, India, and Egypt, in order to study the occult. Although many considered her a 56) <u>fake throughout</u> her lifetime she was surrounded by faithful believers, including such influential persons as British statesman Allen O. Hume and Swedish countess Constance Wachtmeister. To this day, followers commemorate the date of her 57) <u>death calling</u> May 8, "White Lotus Day."

54. a. Blavatsky: born
    b. Blavatsky—born
    c. Blavatsky, born
    d. Blavatsky. Born
    e. correct as it is

55. a. countries, including
    b. countries: including
    c. countries. Including
    d. countries including
    e. correct as it is

56. a. fake, throughout
    b. fake. Throughout
    c. fake: throughout
    d. fake; throughout
    e. correct as it is

57. a. death. Calling
    b. death, calling
    c. death: calling
    d. death; calling
    e. correct as it is

Questions 58–61 are based on the following passage. First read the passage, and then choose the answer that shows the best capitalization and punctuation for each underlined part.

January 2, 2002

Carole Kelly
407 Willow Way
Iowa City, Iowa 52245

Bill **58)** <u>Sherman, general manager</u>
Bill's Garage Door Opener Company
1297 Kentucky Way
Iowa City, Iowa 52240

Dear **59)** <u>Mr. Sherman;</u>

I wish to complain about the door opener you installed in my garage on December 18, 2001. On January 1, **60)** <u>2002 at 10:00 P.M. I</u> returned home from dinner at The Cooperage a restaurant in downtown Iowa City. When I attempted to enter my garage, the device you installed **61)** <u>malfunctioned and my</u> car was damaged. I hope you will make restitution without my having to take legal action.

Sincerely yours,

Carole Kelly

58. a. Sherman, general Manager
  b. sherman, General Manager
  c. Sherman, General Manager
  d. Sherman, General manager
  e. correct as is

59. a. Dear Mr. Sherman.
  b. Dear, Mr. sherman,
  c. dear Mr. Sherman:
  d. Dear Mr. Sherman:
  e. correct as it is

60. a. 2002 at: 3:00 P.M., I
  b. 2002 at 300 P.M., I
  c. 2002 at, 3:00 P.M., I
  d. 2002, at 3:00 P.M. I
  e. correct as it is

61. a. malfunctioned, and my
  b. malfunctioned: and my
  c. malfunctioned? And my
  d. malfunctioned and, my
  e. correct as it is

S · E · C · T · I · O · N

SENTENCE STRUCTURE

A sentence is like a Christmas present: Assembly is always required. Fortunately, the instructions are fairly basic. Every sentence must have at least a **subject** and a **predicate**. The subject is the focus of the sentence; it is the who or the what the sentence is about. The predicate describes the subject; it explains what the subject is or what the subject is doing. The completed idea is called a **clause**, and it is the building block of all sentences.

First, you have to know these terms:

✓ **Independent clause:** a clause that expresses a complete thought. →*Monica walked on the grass.*

✓ **Dependent (subordinate) clause:** a clause that does not express a complete thought. →*Though it was wet*

✓ **A complete thought** →Though it was wet, Monica walked on the grass.

✓ **Essential clause:** a dependent clause that is necessary to the basic meaning of the completed sentence. →*who are pregnant*

   Women who are pregnant can crave salty or sweet foods.

✓ **Nonessential clause:** a dependent clause that is not necessary to the basic meaning of the completed sentence. →*who growls whenever the phone rings*

   Elmo, who growls whenever the phone rings, tried to attack the vacuum cleaner.

✓ **Phrase:** a group of words that lack either a subject or a predicate.→*In early spring*
   In early spring, I notice a change in people's attitudes.

✓ **Appositive:** a phrase that makes a preceding noun or pronoun clearer or more definite by explaining or identifying it.→*rice pudding and fruit salad*
   Candice's grandfather brought her favorite desserts, rice pudding and fruit salad.

✓ *Fragment:* a phrase punctuated like a sentence even though it does not express a complete thought.→ *Timothy saw the car. And ran.*

✓ **Coordinating Conjunction:** a word that when preceded by a comma or a semi colon joins two independent and equal clauses. (*and, but, so, or, for, nor, yet*)→*Dorothy had a beautiful rose garden, and her yard was a profusion of color every summer.*

✓ **Subordinating Conjunction:** a word that makes a clause a dependent clause. (*after, although, as, because, before, if, once, since, than, that, though, unless, until, when, whenever, where, wherever, while*)→*After the accident, mourners covered the beaches nearest to the tragedy with roses.*

✓ **Conjunctive Adverb:** a word that introduces a relationship between two independent clauses. (*accordingly, besides, consequently, furthermore, hence, however, instead, moreover, nevertheless, otherwise, then, therefore, thus*)→*On Tuesdays, I play racquetball; otherwise, I would go with you.*

To construct a sentence:

✓ Always have at least one independent clause in the sentence.

✓ Join two independent clauses with a semicolon or a comma and a **conjunction.**→*Chaucer was a narrator, and he was a pilgrim in his* Canterbury Tales.

✓ Do not run two or more independent clauses together without punctuation; that error is appropriately called a **run-on.** Wrong: *Chaucer was a narrator and he was a pilgrim in his* Canterbury Tales.

✓ Do not separate two independent clauses with just a comma; that error is called a **comma splice.** Wrong: *Chaucer was a narrator, he was a pilgrim in his* Canterbury Tales.

✓ Do not use a **conjunctive adverb** (the words *accordingly, besides, consequently, furthermore, hence, however, instead, moreover, nevertheless, otherwise, then, therefore, thus*) like a **conjunction.** Wrong: *Chaucer was a narrator, moreover he was a pilgrim in his* Canterbury Tales.

✓ Use a comma after a conjunctive adverb when it follows a semicolon. (See Conjunctive Adverbs)

✓ Use a comma after introductory words, phrases, and clauses. (See Subordinating Clauses)

✓ Use commas around non-essential clauses. Do not use commas around essential clauses. (See Non Essential and Essential Clauses)

✓ Use commas around appositives. (See Appositives)

✓ Use commas around parenthetical elements (a word or group of words that interrupt a sentence's flow).→*Mrs. Moses, that mean old crone, yelled at little Paula for laughing too loud!*

SET 6 (Answers begin on page 121.)
Fill in the blank with the word that creates the most logical sentence. (Hint: Use a dictionary to determine which words best complete the sentence's meaning.)

62. _____ strip mining is the cheapest method of mining, it is often harmful to the environment.
    a. Besides
    b. Unless
    c. Nevertheless
    d. Although

63. Yori had a bad cold. _____, he decided not to go to the movie with us.
    a. Therefore
    b. Meanwhile
    c. However
    d. Anyway

64. _____ she waited for the bus to arrive, Julia sat on the bench and read her book.
    a. So that
    b. While
    c. Even if
    d. Besides when

65. My mother likes rock music _____ it is played at a low volume.
    a. because
    b. whether
    c. when
    d. as if

66. Joelle's favorite beverages are herb tea and mineral water. Chelsea, _____, drinks only milk or juice.
    a. however
    b. therefore
    c. then
    d. too

67. _____ our low interest rates, you will receive a free gift if you sign up now.
    a. While
    b. Because
    c. In spite of
    d. In addition to

68. Aunt Judy said dinner would be served at 6:30, but we didn't start eating _____ 7:15.
    a. less than
    b. until
    c. about
    d. since

69. My dog Charley is afraid of thunder; _____, when there's a storm I cover his ears.
    a. mainly
    b. yet
    c. moreover
    d. consequently

70. The log cabin quilt was probably designed as a way to give a second life to unwieldy but warm fabrics salvaged _____ suits and coats.
    a. from
    b. in
    c. with
    d. at

71. Sandra Day O'Connor, the first woman to serve on the United States Supreme Court, _____ appointed by President Ronald Reagan in 1981.
   a. she
   b. and
   c. but
   d. was

72. I _____ the speech you gave last Thursday night, but I was in bed with the flu.
   a. will have heard
   b. would hear
   c. might hear
   d. would have heard

73. _____ the Beatles' most popular songs—most of which were written by Lennon and McCartney—are "I Want to Hold Your Hand" and "Hey, Jude."
   a. With
   b. Considering
   c. Among
   d. To

SET 7 (Answers begin on page 122.)
Choose the sentence that best combines the underlined sentences.

74. The airport is called the Glynco Jetport. The airline reservations and travel systems refer to its location as Brunswick, Georgia.
   a. Where the airport is called the Glynco Jetport, the airline reservations and travel systems refer to the location as Brunswick, Georgia.
   b. But the airport is called the Glynco Jetport, the airline reservations and travel systems refer to the location as Brunswick, Georgia.
   c. Even though the airline reservations and travel systems refer to the location as Brunswick, Georgia, the airport is called the Glynco Jetport.
   d. When the airport is called the Glynco Jetport, the airline reservations refer to the location as Brunswick, Georgia, and the travel systems.

75. Plato believed that boys and girls should be given an equal education. This idea is rarely mentioned in textbooks.
   a. Plato believed that boys and girls should be given an equal education, where this idea is rarely mentioned in textbooks.
   b. Plato believed that boys and girls should be given an equal education, an idea that is rarely mentioned in textbooks.
   c. Believing that boys and girls should be given an equal education, Plato's idea is rarely mentioned in textbooks.
   d. Plato believed that boys and girls should be given an equal education, whereupon this idea is rarely mentioned in textbooks.

76. Recently there have been government cutbacks in funds. Experts foresee steady hiring in the government's future.

   a. Despite recent government cutbacks in funds, experts foresee steady hiring in the government's future.

   b. Whereupon recent government cutbacks in funds, experts foresee steady hiring in the government's future.

   c. So that there have been recent government cutbacks in funds, experts foresee steady hiring in the government's future.

   d. Nonetheless there have been recent government cutbacks in funds, experts foresee steady hiring in the government's future.

77. The federal government has diversity of jobs and geographic locations. The federal government offers flexibility in job opportunities that is unmatched in the private sector.

   a. In spite of its diversity of jobs and geographic locations, the federal government offers flexibility in job opportunities that is unmatched in the private sector.

   b. No matter its diversity of jobs and geographic locations, the federal government offers flexibility in job opportunities that is unmatched in the private sector.

   c. Because of its diversity of jobs and geographic locations, the federal government offers flexibility in job opportunities that is unmatched in the private sector.

   d. The federal government has diversity of jobs and geographic locations, so it offers flexibility in job opportunities that is unmatched in the private sector.

78. The Greeks thought that the halcyon, or kingfisher, nested on the sea. All birds nest on land.

   a. Whereupon all birds nest on land, the Greeks thought that the halcyon, or kingfisher, nested on the sea.

   b. The Greeks thought that the halcyon, or kingfisher, nested on the sea, whereas all birds nest on land.

   c. Whenever all birds nest on land, the Greeks thought that the halcyon, or kingfisher, nested on the sea.

   d. The Greeks thought that the halcyon, or kingfisher, nested on the sea, as all birds nest on land.

79. The old brain is called the reptilian brain. It does not know passion, but only stolid obedience to its own genetic dictates.

   a. After the old brain is called the reptilian brain, it does not know passion, but only stolid obedience to its own genetic dictates.

   b. The old brain, called the reptilian brain, does not know passion, but only stolid obedience to its own genetic dictates.

   c. The old brain is called the reptilian brain, whereupon it does not know passion, but only stolid obedience to its own genetic dictates.

   d. Unless the old brain, called the reptilian brain, does not know passion, only stolid obedience to its own genetic dictates.

80. There have been great strides in the practical application of quantum physics in the last decade. We are no closer to actually understanding it than were the physicists of the 1920s.

    a. Unless there have been great strides in the practical application of quantum physics in the last few decades, we are no closer to actually understanding it than were the physicists of the 1920s.

    b. In the last few decades, we are no closer to actually understanding it than were the physicists of the 1920s, until there have been great strides in the practical application of quantum physics.

    c. Although there have been great strides in the practical application of quantum physics in the last few decades, we are no closer to actually understanding it than were the physicists of the 1920s.

    d. In the last few decades, if there have been great strides in the practical application of quantum physics we are no closer to actually understanding it than were the physicists of the 1920s.

81. The wisdom of the hedgehog is applauded in medieval bestiaries. The hedgehog builds a nest with two exits and, when in danger, rolls itself into a prickly ball.

    a. The wisdom of the hedgehog is applauded in medieval bestiaries, while the hedgehog builds a nest with two exits and, when in danger, rolls itself into a prickly ball.

    b. The hedgehog builds a nest with two exits and, when in danger, rolls itself into a prickly ball, so its wisdom is applauded in medieval bestiaries.

    c. The hedgehog builds a nest with two exits and, when in danger, rolls itself into a prickly ball, but its wisdom is applauded in medieval bestiaries.

    d. Its wisdom applauded in medieval bestiaries, the hedgehog builds a nest with two exits and, when in danger, rolls itself into a prickly ball

82. Some people believe fairy tales are merely children's stories. Some people believe fairy tales carry important psychological truths for adults.

    a. When some believe they carry important psychological truths for adults, some people believe fairy tales are merely children's stories.

    b. Some people believe fairy tales are merely children's stories, whereupon some believe they carry important psychological truths for adults.

    c. Because some believe fairy tales carry important psychological truths for adults, some people believe fairy tales are merely children's stories.

    d. Some people believe fairy tales are merely children's stories, yet some believe they carry important psychological truths for adults.

83. <u>Most species of the bacterium Streptococcus are harmless. Some species of Streptococcus are dangerous pathogens.</u>

a. Whereas most species of the bacterium Streptococcus are harmless, some are dangerous pathogens.

b. Since most species of the bacterium Streptococcus are harmless, some are dangerous pathogens.

c. As most species of the bacterium Streptococcus are harmless, some are dangerous pathogens.

d. Because most species of the bacterium Streptococcus are harmless, some are dangerous pathogens.

84. <u>The man nodded politely. His expression was bewildered.</u>

a. Nodding politely, the man's expression was bewildered.

b. The man nodded politely his expression was bewildered.

c. The man nodded politely, his expression bewildered.

d. The man nodded politely, since his expression was bewildered.

SET 8 (Answers begin on page 123.)
Choose the sentence that best combines the under-lined sentences.

85. <u>Watching a TV show is a passive behavior. Playing a computer game is an interactive one.</u>

a. Watching a TV show is a passive behavior, or playing a computer game is an interactive one.

b. Watching a TV show is a passive behavior, for playing a computer game is an interactive one.

c. Watching a TV show is a passive behavior, but playing a computer game is an interactive one.

d. Being that playing a computer game is an interactive one, watching a TV show is a passive behavior.

86. <u>Socrates taught that we should question everything, even the law. He was both greatly loved and profoundly hated.</u>

a. That he was both greatly loved and profoundly hated, Socrates taught that we should question everything, even the law.

b. Socrates taught that we should question everything, even the law, so he was both greatly loved and profoundly hated.

c. Socrates taught that we should question everything, even the law, which he was both greatly loved and profoundly hated.

d. Socrates taught that we should question everything, even the law, for he was both greatly loved and profoundly hated.

87. Sailors are said to catch albatrosses with baited hooks let down into the ship's wake. To kill the albatross was thought to be bad luck, so they were released immediately.

a. Sailors are said to catch albatrosses with baited hooks and let them down into the ship's wake, then release them again, for to kill the albatross was thought to be bad luck.

b. With baited hooks let down into the ship's wake, sailors are said to catch albatrosses then release them again, so to kill the albatross was thought to be bad luck.

c. Sailors are said to catch albatrosses with baited hooks let down into the ship's wake, then release them again, or to kill the albatross was thought to be bad luck.

d. To kill the albatross was thought to be bad luck, so sailors are said to catch albatrosses with baited hooks let down into the ship's wake, only to release them immediately.

88. The symptoms of diabetes often develop gradually and are hard to identify at first. Nearly half of all people with diabetes do not know they have it.

a. The symptoms of diabetes often develop gradually and are hard to identify at first, so nearly half of all people with diabetes do not know they have it.

b. The symptoms of diabetes often develop gradually and are hard to identify at first, yet nearly half of all people with diabetes do not know they have it.

c. Nearly half of all people with diabetes do not know they have it, and the symptoms

of diabetes often develop gradually and are hard to identify at first.

d. The symptoms of diabetes often develop gradually for nearly half of all people with diabetes do not know they have it and are hard to identify at first.

89. The French philosopher Voltaire was greatly respected. Voltaire spent almost a year imprisoned in the Bastille.

a. The French philosopher Voltaire was greatly respected, so he spent almost a year imprisoned in the Bastille.

b. The French philosopher Voltaire was greatly respected with almost a year imprisoned in the Bastille.

c. The French philosopher Voltaire was greatly respected, or he spent almost a year imprisoned in the Bastille.

d. The French philosopher Voltaire was greatly respected, yet he spent almost a year imprisoned in the Bastille.

90. I must buy some new shoes to wear to the prom. My date, Donnie, will be upset if I wear my flip-flops.

a. Unless my date, Donnie, will be upset if I wear my flip-flops, I must buy some new shoes to wear to the prom.

b. I must buy some new shoes to wear to the prom, and my date, Donnie, will be upset if I wear my flip-flops.

c. I must buy some new shoes to wear to the prom, for my date, Donnie, will be upset if I wear my flip-flops.

d. My date, Donnie, will be upset if I wear my flip-flops while I must buy some new shoes to wear to the prom.

91. <u>Sylvia is loaded with money. She can afford that trip to Silver Dollar City.</u>
  a. Sylvia is loaded with money, or she can afford that trip to Silver Dollar City.
  b. Sylvia is loaded with money, but she can afford that trip to Silver Dollar City.
  c. Sylvia is loaded with money, so she can afford that trip to Silver Dollar City.
  d. Sylvia is loaded with money, yet she can afford that trip to Silver Dollar City.

92. <u>The rules of statistics say that it is possible for all the air in a room to move to one corner. This is extremely unlikely.</u>
  a. The rules of statistics say that it is possible for all the air in a room to move to one corner, or this is extremely unlikely.
  b. The rules of statistics say that it is possible for all the air in a room to move to one corner, but this is extremely unlikely.
  c. This is extremely unlikely in that the rules of statistics say that it is possible for all the air in a room to move to one corner.
  d. For all the air in a room to move to one corner, this is extremely unlikely, according to the rules of statistics saying that it is possible.

93. <u>I must buy my dog a new license. If I don't, I will have to pay a fine.</u>
  a. I must buy my dog a new license, and I will have to pay a fine.
  b. I must buy my dog a new license; I will have to pay a fine.
  c. Unless I buy my dog a new license, I will have to pay a fine.
  d. I will have to pay a fine since I must buy my dog a new license.

94. <u>Bats are not rodents. Bats bear a surface resemblance to a winged mouse.</u>
  a. Bats are not rodents, although they do bear a resemblance to a winged mouse.
  b. Bats are not rodents that they bear a surface resemblance to a winged mouse.
  c. Bats are not rodents, when they bear a surface resemblance to a winged mouse.
  d. Bats are not rodents, if they bear a surface resemblance to a winged mouse.

95. <u>Art is not only found in the museum or concert hall. Art can be found in the expressive behavior of ordinary people, as well.</u>
  a. Art can be found not only in the museum or concert hall, and it can be found in the expressive behavior of ordinary people, as well
  b. In the museum or concert hall, art can be found not only there and in the expressive behavior of ordinary people, as well.
  c. Although in the expressive behavior of ordinary people, as well, art can be found not only in the museum or concert hall.
  d. Art can be found not only in the museum or concert hall, but in the expressive behavior of ordinary people, as well.

96. <u>In lucid dreams, the dreamer knows she is dreaming. It gives her a sense of unlimited freedom.</u>
- a. In lucid dreams, the dreamer knows she is dreaming, although it gives her a sense of unlimited freedom.
- b. In lucid dreams, the dreamer knows she is dreaming while it gives her a sense of unlimited freedom.
- c. In lucid dreams, the dreamer knows she is dreaming, where it gives her a sense of unlimited freedom.
- d. In lucid dreams, the dreamer knows she is dreaming, which gives her a sense of unlimited freedom.

SET 9 (Answers begin on page 123.)
Choose the sentence that best combines the underlined sentences.

97. <u>He did not return from his camping trip until 6:00 A.M. We were all frantic with worry.</u>
- a. He did not return from his camping trip until 6:00 A.M.; however we were all frantic with worry.
- b. While we were all frantic with worry, he did not return from his camping trip until 6:00 A.M.
- c. He did not return from his camping trip until 6:00 A.M., whether we were all frantic with worry.
- d. Because he did not return from his camping trip until 6:00 A.M., we were all frantic with worry.

98. <u>Everyone likes Earl. I think he is sneaky.</u>
- a. That everyone likes Earl, I think he is sneaky.
- b. Everyone likes Earl, whereas I think he is sneaky.
- c. Everyone likes Earl, when I think he is sneaky.
- d. Everyone likes Earl, or I think he is sneaky.

99. <u>Maya is an intelligent woman. Maya cannot read or write.</u>
- a. Maya cannot read or write, while she is an intelligent woman.
- b. Maya cannot read or write and is an intelligent woman.
- c. Although Maya cannot read or write, she is an intelligent woman.
- d. Being an intelligent woman, Maya cannot read or write.

100. <u>This area of the country is called "tornado alley." Many tornadoes roar through here every spring.</u>
- a. Many tornadoes roar through here every spring, while this area of the country is called "tornado alley."
- b. Many tornadoes roar through here every spring, but this area of the country is called "tornado alley."
- c. Many tornadoes roar through here every spring; therefore, this area of the country is called "tornado alley."
- d. This area of the country is called "tornado alley;" meanwhile, many tornadoes roar through here every spring.

101. The owl parrot looks like a bird of prey. The owl parrot feeds on vegetable matter.

a. The owl parrot looks like a bird of prey; however, it feeds on vegetable matter.

b. Feeding on vegetable matter, the owl parrot looks like a bird of prey.

c. Looking like a bird of prey, the owl parrot feeds on vegetable matter.

d. The owl parrot feeds on vegetable matter, and it looks like a bird of prey.

102. Mr. Markley has an unpleasant personality. Mr. Markley is a crook.

a. Mr. Markley has an unpleasant personality, and furthermore he's a crook.

b. Mr. Markley has an unpleasant personality, although he is a crook.

c. While he is a crook, Mr. Markley has an unpleasant personality.

d. Being a crook, Mr. Markley has an unpleasant personality.

103. We never had food fights in our cafeteria or cut classes. We did smoke in the Girls' Room.

a. We never had food fights in our cafeteria or cut classes, but we did smoke in the Girls' Room.

b. Because we never had food fights in our cafeteria or cut classes, we smoked in the Girls' Room.

c. We never had food fights in our cafeteria or cut classes, so we did smoke in the Girls' Room.

d. We never had food fights in our cafeteria or cut classes and smoke in the Girls' Room.

104. The rattling of chains in the dungeon of an ancient castle surely must be frightening. It cannot be as frightening as the eerie sensation of watching a horror movie alone at midnight.

a. The rattling of chains in the dungeon of an ancient castle surely must be frightening, so it cannot be as frightening as the eerie sensation of watching a horror movie alone at midnight.

b. The rattling of chains in the dungeon of an ancient castle surely must be frightening, and it cannot be as frightening as the eerie sensation of watching a horror movie alone at midnight.

c. The rattling of chains in the dungeon of an ancient castle surely must be frightening, but it cannot be as frightening as the eerie sensation of watching a horror movie alone at midnight.

d. The rattling of chains in the dungeon of an ancient castle surely must be frightening, or it cannot be as frightening as the eerie sensation of watching a horror movie alone at midnight.

105. I was afraid of the dark. I always slept with the light on.

a. I was afraid of the dark, to where I always slept with the light on.

b. Although I was afraid of the dark, I always slept with the light on.

c. I always slept with the light on being afraid of the dark.

d. I was afraid of the dark, so I always slept with the light on.

106. Insomnia does not usually begin as a physical problem. It can affect one's physical health.

   a. Insomnia is not usually a physical problem; therefore, it can affect one's physical health.

   b. Insomnia is not usually a physical problem, yet it can affect one's physical health.

   c. Insomnia not usually a physical problem can affect one's physical health.

   d. Insomnia is not usually a physical problem, so it can affect one's physical health.

107. True narcolepsy is the sudden and irresistible onset of sleep during waking hours. True narcolepsy is extremely dangerous.

   a. While true narcolepsy is the sudden and irresistible onset of sleep during waking hours and is extremely dangerous.

   b. The sudden and irresistible onset of sleep during waking hours, which is true narcolepsy but extremely dangerous.

   c. True narcolepsy is the sudden and irresistible onset of sleep during waking hours, yet narcolepsy is extremely dangerous.

   d. True narcolepsy is the sudden and irresistible onset of sleep during waking hours, and it is extremely dangerous.

108. There has been much interest in dreams throughout the ages. The empirical, scientific study of dreams is relatively new.

   a. Despite much interest in dreams throughout the ages, the empirical, scientific study of dreams being relatively new.

   b. There has been much interest in dreams throughout the ages, yet the empirical, scientific study of dreams is relatively new.

   c. While much interest in dreams throughout the ages, although the empirical, scientific study of dreams is relatively new.

   d. There has been much interest in dreams throughout the ages, for the empirical, scientific study of dreams is relatively new.

SET 10 (Answers begin on page 124.)
Replace the underlined portion with the phrase that best completes the sentence. If the sentence is correct as is, choose **a.**

109. I look forward to meeting with you and having the opportunity to show you our new products.

   a. I look forward to meeting with you and having

   b. I will look forward to our meeting and having

   c. As I look forward to our meeting and to have

   d. I look forward to meeting with you and have

   e. Looking forward to our meeting and hoping to have

110. <u>For a wide variety of different reasons, more and more people</u> are making the choice to take public transportation.

    a. For a wide variety of different reasons, more and more people

    b. For a variety of many reasons, much more people

    c. For a number of reasons, more people

    d. More people, for various different reasons,

    e. Lots of people, for many numerous reasons

111. <u>The likelihood</u> of a region's experiencing an earthquake can be estimated, earthquakes cannot be accurately predicted.

    a. The likelihood

    b. Although the likelihood

    c. Since the likelihood

    d. In fact, the likelihood

    e. Knowing that the likelihood

112. Most of a human tooth is made up of a substance known as <u>dentin, which is located</u> directly below the enamel.

    a. dentin, which is located

    b. dentin, and which is located

    c. dentin but located

    d. dentin, which it is located

    e. dentin, that its location is

113. Jackson Pollock, <u>a twentieth-century American painter, is well-known and renowned for creating</u> abstract paintings by dripping paint on canvas.

    a. a twentieth-century American painter, is well-known and renowned for creating

    b. an American painter who lived and painted in the twentieth century, is well-known for the creation of

    c. renowned and prominent, was known as a twentieth-century American painter for creating

    d. he is an American painter famous and renowned for creating

    e. a twentieth-century American painter, is famous for creating

114. <u>Having stopped twice to get gas, this was the cause of our late arrival.</u>

    a. Having stopped twice to get gas, this was the cause of our late arrival.

    b. After stopping twice to get gas, our late arrival was anticipated.

    c. Because we stopped twice to get gas, we arrived late.

    d. We arrived late twice stopping to get gas.

    e. Arriving late, we stopped twice to get gas.

115. Because of the need for security, <u>all employees must take reasonable precautions to safeguard</u> any paper or electronic copies of our customers' accounts.

   a. all employees must take reasonable precautions to safeguard

   b. all employees who work here must be cautious and careful to safeguard

   c. employees must be reasonable in safeguarding and protecting

   d. workers and employees must take reasonable measures to protect

   e. all workers must take reasonable precautions and safeguards in order to protect

116. <u>Beside its use in medicine,</u> lasers have many industrial uses.

   a. Beside its use in medicine,

   b. Beside medicine,

   c. In addition also to its medical applications,

   d. Besides its use in medicine,

   e. Besides your using it in medicine,

117. The movie *Titanic* was <u>a big hit in the U.S. like Europe.</u>

   a. a big hit in the U.S. like Europe.

   b. as well a big hit in Europe as it was in the U.S.

   c. just as big a hit in the U.S. than in Europe.

   d. as big a hit in the U.S. as it was in Europe.

   e. a big hit as well as in both Europe and the U.S.

118. We sat down to a five-course <u>meal, and after we had eaten, the dog</u> appeared in the doorway and began to beg.

   a. meal, and after we had eaten, the dog

   b. meal, and after we had eaten the dog

   c. meal and after we had eaten, the dog,

   d. meal; and, after we had eaten, the dog

   e. meal and after we had eaten the dog

119. <u>Running toward it as the bus drove off, leaving Xavier and me standing helplessly on the sidewalk.</u>

   a. Running toward it as the bus drove off, leaving Xavier and me standing helplessly on the sidewalk.

   b. While running toward it and watching the bus drive off, which left Xavier and me standing helplessly on the sidewalk.

   c. Left helplessly standing on the sidewalk after Xavier and me ran toward the bus and watched it as it drove off.

   d. As we ran toward it, the bus drove off, leaving Xavier and me standing helplessly on the sidewalk.

   e. After having run toward it, the bus driving off and leaving Xavier and me on the sidewalk, watching helplessly.

SET 11 (Answers begin on page 125.)
Replace the underlined portion with the phrase that best completes the sentence. If the sentence is correct as is, choose **a.**

120. When making a chocolate torte, <u>only the best ingredients should be used.</u>
    a. only the best ingredients should be used.
    b. you should use only the best ingredients.
    c. the best ingredients only should be used.
    d. one should have used only the best ingredients.
    e. using only the best ingredients is essential.

121. With her book *Coming of Age in Samoa*, anthropologist Margaret Mead emphasized the role of culture, <u>rather than biology, in shaping human behavior.</u>
    a. rather than biology, in shaping human behavior.
    b. rather than biology with shaping human behavior.
    c. somewhat better than biology to shape human behavior.
    d. in shaping human behavior, and not biology.
    e. in shaping human behavior over biology.

122. This was the fifth <u>of the five speeches the mayor gave during this the month of May.</u>
    a. This was the fifth of the five speeches the mayor gave during this the month of May.
    b. Of the five speeches the mayor gave during May, this was the fifth one.
    c. Thus far during the month of May, the mayor gave five speeches and this was the fifth.
    d. This fifth speech of the mayor's given during the month of May was one of five speeches.
    e. This was the fifth speech the mayor has given during the month of May.

123. An American poet of the nineteenth century, <u>Walt Whitman's collection of poems, *Leaves of Grass*,</u> celebrates nature and individualism.
    a. Walt Whitman's collection of poems, *Leaves of Grass*,
    b. *Leaves of Grass*, a collection of poems by Walt Whitman,
    c. a collection of poems, *Leaves of Grass*, by Walt Whitman,
    d. Walt Whitman published poems, collected as *Leaves of Grass*, that
    e. Walt Whitman, published a collection of poems entitled *Leaves of Grass*, that

124. We loved our trip to the <u>desert where you could see</u> the tall cactus, the blooming flowers, and the little desert animals.
    a. desert where you could see
    b. desert; you could see
    c. desert; where we saw
    d. desert; we saw
    e. desert in that you saw

125. <u>Opposite in what many financial analysts had predicted,</u> the stock market rose by twenty-two points this month.
    a. Opposite in what many financial analysts had predicted,
    b. Contrary to the predictions of many financial analysts,
    c. As against the predictions of many financial analysts,
    d. Contrasting of many financial analysts' predictions,
    e. Contrary with what many financial analysts predicted,

126. A standardized extract made from the leaves of the ginkgo biloba tree <u>is proving to be effective in treating</u> mild to moderate Alzheimer's disease.
    a. is proving to be effective in treating
    b. has shown its proof of effectiveness with treating
    c. may have proven effective treatment for
    d. is effectively proving in treating
    e. have given a proven effectiveness in the treatment of

127. The citizens' action committee has accused the city counsel members <u>with being careless with the spending of</u> the taxpayers' money.
    a. with being careless with the spending of
    b. as to carelessness in the spending of
    c. of carelessness in the spending of
    d. of careless spending to
    e. with spending carelessly of

128. Aspirin was exclusively known <u>as a painkiller until the time when cardiologists began prescribing it as a preventative for</u> heart attacks.
    a. as a painkiller until the time when cardiologists began prescribing it as a preventative for
    b. to be a painkiller since when cardiologists prescribed it to be a prevention for
    c. as a way to kill and stop pain until cardiologists began to prescribe it as a method for the prevention of
    d. as a painkiller until cardiologists began prescribing it as a preventative for
    e. to be a painkiller up to when cardiologists prescribed its preventative for

129. The news reporter who <u>had been covering the story suddenly became ill, and I was called</u> to take her place.
    a. had been covering the story suddenly became ill, and I was called
    b. was covering the story suddenly becomes ill, and they called me
    c. is covering the story suddenly becomes ill, and I was called
    d. would have been covering the story suddenly became ill, and I am called
    e. covers the story, suddenly became ill, and they called me

130. Lee Iacocca, the son of Italian immigrants, he worked his way to the top of the Ford Motor Company and later rescued Chrysler Corporation.
  a. Lee Iacocca, the son of Italian immigrants, he
  b. Lee Iacocca, being the son of Italian immigrants,
  c. As he was the son of Italian immigrants, Lee Iacocca
  d. The son of Italian immigrants, Lee Iacocca
  e. Lee Iacocca, the son of Italian immigrants, and he

131. The troposphere is the lowest layer of Earth's atmosphere, it extends from ground level to an altitude of seven to ten miles.
  a. atmosphere, it extends
  b. atmosphere of which it extends
  c. atmosphere. Extending
  d. atmosphere, and extending
  e. atmosphere; it extends

132. Along with your membership to our health club and two months of free personal training.
  a. Along with your membership to our health club, and
  b. Along with your membership to our health club you receive
  c. With your membership to our health club,
  d. In addition to your membership to our health club being
  e. Added to your membership to our health club,

133. Our contention is that a body of common knowledge shared by literate Americans of the late twentieth century and that this knowledge can be defined.
  a. Our contention is that a body of common knowledge shared by
  b. To contend that a body of common knowledge is shared by
  c. We contend that we share a body of common knowledge in
  d. That a common body of knowledge is shared is our contention with
  e. It is our contention that a body of common knowledge is shared by

134. Whether they earn a B.S. degree, chemical engineers are almost guaranteed a job.
  a. Whether they earn
  b. If they earn
  c. If earning
  d. To earn
  e. Since earning

SET 12 (Answers begin on page 126.)
Choose the sentence that is NOT correctly written or is unclear. If all sentences are correct, choose answer **d**.

135. a. We urged her to run for public office.
  b. Mr. Simmons did not believe the story we told him.
  c. The train pulling away from the station.
  d. No mistakes.

136.
a. Our class took a field trip, going to the art museum.
b. There are rocky cliffs along the coast.
c. We saw Dr. Mason because our doctor was on vacation.
d. No mistakes.

137.
a. They're planning to drive to Vermont today.
b. When will you teach me to play the guitar?
c. There's no reason to stay up so late.
d. No mistakes.

138.
a. Make sure your seatbelt is fastened.
b. I'm afraid of spiders George is too.
c. Yes, I will bring the dessert.
d. No mistakes.

139.
a. After you left, I took the dog for a walk.
b. For the first time, I understood what he was talking about.
c. We visited the house where President George Washington lived last fall.
d. No mistakes.

140.
a. Sandra Day O'Connor was the first woman to serve on the U.S. Supreme Court.
b. The judge met with both attorneys in his chambers.
c. Which of the Beatles' songs do you like best?
d. No mistakes.

141.
a. They traveled south and hiked in the desert.
b. "Don't shout at me," she yelled back.
c. Joshua enters lots of contests, unless he knows he can't win.
d. No mistakes.

142.
a. Turn off that television it's time for dinner!
b. The dancers' shoes were all lined up against the wall.
c. Have you ever visited Smokey Mountain National Park?
d. No mistakes.

143.
a. I'm taking a class in West Indian literature.
b. The people in the park, including all the children on the swings.
c. Andrea likes my cheesecake better than Aunt Lydia's.
d. No mistakes.

144.
a. Where's my blue jacket?
b. The prizes were awarded to Juan and me.
c. After midnight, you will turn into a pumpkin.
d. No mistakes.

145.
a. The muffins cost more than the bread does.
b. Roberta and I were in the same watercolor class.
c. The temperature was colder today than it was yesterday.
d. No mistakes.

146.
a. Indira sometimes wears her beautiful sari.
b. Lyle went shopping, and that he forgot his wallet.
c. His shoes are just like mine.
d. No mistakes.

SET 13 (Answers begin on page 126.)
Choose the sentence that expresses the idea most clearly.

147. a. For three weeks the Merryville Fire Chief received taunting calls from an arsonist, who would not say where he intended to set the next fire.
   b. The Merryville Fire Chief received taunting calls from an arsonist, but he would not say where he intended to set the next fire, for three weeks.
   c. He would not say where he intended to set the next fire, but for three weeks the Merryville Fire Chief received taunting calls from an arsonist.
   d. The Merryville Fire Chief received taunting calls from an arsonist for three weeks, not saying where he intended to set the next fire.

148. a. There is no true relationship between ethics and the law.
   b. Ethics and the law having no true relationship.
   c. Between ethics and the law, no true relationship.
   d. Ethics and the law is no true relationship.

149. a. Some people say jury duty is a nuisance that just takes up their precious time and that we don't get paid enough.
   b. Some people say jury duty is a nuisance that just takes up your precious time and that one doesn't get paid enough.
   c. Some people say jury duty is a nuisance that just takes up precious time and that doesn't pay enough.
   d. Some people say jury duty is a nuisance that just takes up our precious time and that they don't get paid enough.

150. a. As soon as she realized that the hurricane was going to strike, the mayor told the residents to evacuate the city.
   b. As soon as she realized that the hurricane was going to strike, the city residents were told to evacuate by the mayor.
   c. As soon as she realized that the hurricane was going to strike, the mayor tells the city residents of her decision to evacuate.
   d. As soon as she realized that the hurricane was going to strike, the residents of the city were told to evacuate by the mayor.

151. a. A sharpshooter for many years, a pea could be shot off a person's shoulder from 70 yards away by Miles Johnson.
   b. A sharpshooter for many years, Miles Johnson could shoot a pea off a person's shoulder from 70 yards away.
   c. A sharpshooter for many years, from 70 yards away off a person's shoulder Miles Johnson could have shot a pea.
   d. A sharpshooter for many years, Miles Johnson could shoot from 70 yards away off a person's shoulder a pea.

152. a. By the time they are in the third or fourth grade, the eyes of most children in the United States are tested.

b. Most children by the time they are in the United States have their eyes tested in the third or fourth grade.

c. Most children in the United States have their eyes tested by the time they are in the third or fourth grade.

d. In the United States by the time of third or fourth grade, there is testing of the eyes of most children.

153. a. Ultraviolet radiation levels are 60 percent higher at 8,500 feet from the sun than they are at sea level, according to researchers.

b. Researchers have found from the sun ultraviolet radiation levels 60 percent higher, they say, at 8,500 feet than at sea level.

c. Researchers have found that ultraviolet radiation levels from the sun are 60 percent higher at 8,500 feet than they are at sea level.

d. At 8,500 feet researchers have found that ultraviolet radiation levels are 60 percent higher from sea level with the sun's rays.

S·E·C·T·I·O·N

AGREEMENT 3

Agreement is a very important step in constructing a coherent sentence. There are three basic agreements in a sentence: subject-verb agreement, tense agreement, and antecedent-pronoun agreement.

First, you have to know the definition of a verb:

✓ **Verb:** a word or group of words describing the action or the state of being of a subject.

SUBJECT-VERB AGREEMENT

✓ If the subject is singular, the verb is singular; if the subject is plural, the verb is plural→*Mrs. Hendrickson feeds the birds every day.* Or: *The Hendricksons feed the birds every day.*

✓ Subjects joined by *and* are plural and receive a plural verb→*Jolie and Lara swim together every Thursday.*

✓ Subjects joined by *or* or *nor* adopt the singularity or plurality of the last subject; accordingly, the verb matches it→*Either that cat or those dogs have been eating my snacks!*

PRONOUN-ANTECEDENT AGREEMENT

✓ *Each, either, neither, anybody, anyone, everybody, everyone, no one, nobody, one, somebody,* and *someone* are singular pronouns and receive singular verbs.

✓ *Both, few, many,* and *several* are plural pronouns and receive plural verbs.

✓ *All, any, most, none,* and *some* can be singular or plural pronouns, depending on their use. These pronouns can receive plural or singular verbs.

✓ Do not be confused by words or phrases that follow a subject that are not the subject→*One of the chairs is damaged.*

His work, one of the many works exhibited here today, is refreshingly naive.

TENSE AGREEMENT

✓ Maintain one tense in a complete thought: past tense or present tense.→

Incorrect: *In the game of hide and seek, Bobby chased Mary and tag her from behind.*

Correct: *In the game of hide and seek, Bobby chased Mary and tagged her from behind.*

Incorrect: *Dusk had just settled when I see a fawn timidly step onto the beach.*

Correct: *Dusk had just settled when I saw a fawn timidly step onto the beach.*

Do not use *of* in place of *have.*

You cannot avoid pronouns. *Pronouns* substitute for nouns. Instead of saying, "Because Janie was late, Janie hopped on Janie's moped, and Janie raced to the wedding," you would say, "Because Janie was late, *she* hopped on *her* moped, and *she* raced to the wedding."

In this section you will not only clarify ambiguous pronouns and assure pronoun antecedent agreement, you will also grapple with contractions. All too often, certain pronouns and contractions are confused. "The file cabinet drawer snagged on an overstuffed folder; *it's* now stuck just before *its* halfway point." *It's* is a contraction meaning *it is* while *its* is a possessive pronoun meaning the drawer's halfway point. The only visual difference between the two is an apostrophe neatly inserted between the *t* and the *s* in the contraction.

DO YOU KNOW THESE TERMS?

✓ **Antecedent:** In the example above, Janie is the specific noun that *she* and *her* replace; so Janie is the *antecedent.* The presence of the antecedent in a sentence is as important as which pronouns substitute for it.

✓ **Contractions:** When two words are made into one by omitting letters and using an apostrophe to highlight the omission—that's a contraction.

✓ **Subjective, Objective and Possessive Cases:** Persons or things (nouns) acting on other things are subjects. Pronouns that refer to these subjects are in the subjective case (I, you, he, she, we, they, who). Persons or things acted upon (in other words, they are not performing the action) are objects. Pronouns that refer to these objects are in the objective case (Me, you, him, her, us, them, whom). Subjects or objects that claim ownership of something are possessors. Pronouns that claim their possessions are in the possessive case (my, your, his, her, our, your, whose).

✓ **AVOID AMBIGUOUS PRONOUN REFERENCES.** The antecedent that a pronoun refers to must be clearly stated and in close proximity to its pronoun.

If more subjects than one are present, indicate which subject is the antecedent.→*When Katherine and Melissa left for England, she promised to write me about all their adventures.* Who is *she*? Katherine or Melissa?

PRONOUNS SHOULD

✓ Agree in number with their antecedent: Singular antecedents use singular pronouns, and plural antecedents use plural pronouns.

✓ *Compound antecedents* joined by *and* use plural pronouns.→*A horse and a donkey make a mule.* Even though the horse and the donkey are singular subjects, together they create one plural subject.

✓ *Compound antecedents* joined by *or* or *nor* use pronouns that agree with the nearest antecedent.→ *Neither my one cat nor my four dogs are as difficult to maintain as my one pet fish.*

✓ *Collective nouns* use singular pronouns unless it is obvious that every person or thing in the group act individually.→*The company mandated a universal naptime for all its employees. They felt workers could sustain productivity longer into the afternoon if they rested in the early afternoon.* Unless it is a one-person operation, a company usually employs many people. However, it is treated like a singular noun. In the first sentence the singular pronoun *it* substitutes for *company*. In the second sentence, individuals in the company feel separately, and so the plural pronoun *they* replaces the subject.

✓ Persons receive the pronouns *who, whom,* or *whose,* not *that* or *which.*

✓ After *is, are, was,* or *were* use the subjective case.

✓ Pronouns preceding or following *infinitive verbs* (the plain form of a verb preceded by *to*) take the objective case.→*Billy Jean begged him to play catch, but he did not want to play ball with her at that moment.* In the first clause *him* is the subject; in the second clause *her* is an object. Despite their difference, both take the objective case because of the infinitive *to play.*

SET 14 (Answers begin on page 127.)

For the following questions, choose the underlined part of the sentence that contains a grammatical error. If there are no errors, choose answer **e**.

154. I think Luis must <u>of missed</u> the <u>bus because</u> he <u>is always</u> on time <u>for</u> every event. <u>No error.</u>
                    a   b   c   d   e

155. Every decade, a <u>few popular</u> television shows <u>transcends</u> mere <u>cleverness and</u> high ratings <u>to reflect</u> the
                       a   b   c   d

social issues of our times. <u>No error.</u>
                    e

156. <u>Each of</u> the students <u>have had</u> a <u>half-hour</u> conference <u>with</u> his or her guidance counselor. <u>No error.</u>
      a   b   c   d   e

157. Here <u>are</u> one of the two <u>books</u> you <u>left</u> in my car <u>yesterday</u> afternoon. <u>No error.</u>
           a   b   c   d   e

158. Soon after Harry <u>stopped to make</u> a phone <u>call, he</u> realized <u>that</u> he <u>should miss</u> the bus. <u>No error.</u>
                         a   b   c   d   e

159. <u>Someone from</u> the garage phoned <u>to say</u> <u>that</u> the car had been fixed and <u>asking</u> if we would pick it up
       a   b   c   d

by 5:00. <u>No error.</u>
        e

160. In 1963, Betty <u>Friedan's</u> exposé of domesticity, *The Feminine Mystique*, became <u>an immediate</u> bestseller
                a   b   c

<u>and creating</u> a national sensation. <u>No error.</u>
  d   e

161. The staff at the <u>university</u> library <u>deserve</u> recognition for <u>helping to locate</u> the <u>many sources needed</u> for
                a   b   c   d

the successful completion of my doctoral dissertation. <u>No error.</u>
                                          e

162. <u>Homesteaders</u> on the <u>Great Plains</u> had to build homes, find water <u>in a semiarid</u> land, <u>and to learn</u> to
   a   b   c   d

understand the blessings of the environment. <u>No error.</u>
                                e

163. <u>During</u> the winter season, homeowners should change <u>their</u> disposable furnace filters at least once
   a   b

<u>a month; a</u> dirty filter <u>reduce</u> furnace efficiency. <u>No error.</u>
   c   d   e

164. The chief executive <u>officer and</u> the chairman of the board <u>agrees</u> that the new benefit package
                    a   b

<u>should include</u> a dental health plan <u>as well as</u> eye care. <u>No error.</u>
   c   d   e

165. <u>Watching</u> the film, I <u>begun</u> to ask <u>myself</u> why I cared about <u>these characters</u> when I felt such an intense
   a   b   c   d

unease. <u>No error.</u>
      e

SET 15 (Answers begin on page 128.)
Fill in the blank with the correct verb form.

166. On February 27, 1995, the City Fire
Department responded to a blaze that
_____ at the Icarus Publishing Co.
warehouse.
   a. breaks out
   b. will break out
   c. had broken out
   d. is breaking out

167. Gary Talerino and Jennifer O'Brien attended a
dance that the school _____.
   a. sponsors.
   b. will sponsor.
   c. is sponsoring.
   d. sponsored.

168. I am trying to become more skilled at weaving
before winter _____.
   a. arrived
   b. will have arrived
   c. will arrive
   d. arrives

169. We have _____ more of these strange pods
since those people moved in next door.
   a. saw
   b. been seeing
   c. been seen
   d. see

170. While trying to _____ his pet iguana from
a tree, Travis Stevens fell and broke his ankle.
   a. be rescuing
   b. have rescued
   c. rescue
   d. rescuing

171. _____ the baby down carefully.
   a. Put
   b. Putted
   c. Been putting
   d. To put

172. The main problem Jim had _____ too
many parking tickets.
   a. will have been
   b. were
   c. will have
   d. was

173. On Wednesday, Jamal and Jennifer were called
to the principal's office and praised for helping
a student who _____ on the icy sidewalk.
   a. falls
   b. would fall
   c. had fallen
   d. has fallen

174. The people who bought this old lamp at the
auction _____ foolish.
   a. was
   b. were
   c. is
   d. has been

175. The little boy _____ himself down on the
floor and threw a tantrum.
   a. flings
   b. flinged
   c. flung
   d. fling

176. There _____ three different ways to make
perfect pie crust.
   a. is
   b. are
   c. was
   d. being

177. The noise from all the airplanes _____ louder in the afternoon.
  a. gets
  b. get
  c. have gotten
  d. are getting

SET 16 (Answers begin on page 128.)
Replace the underlined words with the phrase that best completes the sentence. If the sentence is correct as is, choose **a**.

178. The words Equal Justice Under Law <u>is carved</u> above the main entrance to the Supreme Court.
  a. is carved
  b. carved
  c. has been carved
  d. are carved
  e. been carved

179. In classical economic theory, the relationship <u>between supply and demand determines</u> the price of a commodity.
  a. between supply and demand determines
  b. among supply and demand determines
  c. among supply and demand determine
  d. between supply and demand determine
  e. with supply and demand determine

180. A corporation created by the federal government during the Great Depression, the Tennessee Valley Authority (TVA) is responsible for <u>flood control, must generate electric power, and soil conservation.</u>
  a. flood control, must generate electric power, and soil conservation.
  b. flood control, generating electric power, and for soil conservation.
  c. controlling floods, generating electric power, and soil conservation.
  d. flood control, the generation of electric power, and soil conservation.
  e. flood control, for the generation of electric power, and conserving the soil.

181. According to traditional Chinese medicine, people with healthy livers <u>are said to be calm and that they possess</u> unerring judgment.
  a. are said to be calm and that they possess
  b. are said to be calm and to possess
  c. said to be calm and possessing
  d. have said to be calm and to possess
  e. are said to be calm and possessive of

182. When the phone <u>is ringing, Jacoby had been writing</u> in his journal.
  a. is ringing, Jacoby had been writing
  b. rings, Jacoby was writing
  c. rang, Jacoby was writing
  d. had rung, Jacoby was writing
  e. rang, Jacoby will be writing

183. <u>To determine the speed of automobiles, radar is often used by the state police.</u>
  a. To determine the speed of automobiles, radar is often used by the state police.
  b. To determine the speed of automobiles, it is often necessary for the state police to use radar.
  c. In determining the speed of automobiles, the use of radar by state police is often employed.
  d. To determine the speed of automobiles, the state police often use radar.
  e. Radar by state police in determining the speed of automobiles is often used.

184. Everyone signed the petition before <u>submitting</u> to the city council.

   a. submitting

   b. one submits it

   c. you submit it

   d. we will submit it

   e. we submitted it

185. I have a cross-training exercise program: <u>I swim laps, play tennis, the weight machines, and bicycle riding.</u>

   a. I swim laps, play tennis, the weight machines, and bicycle riding.

   b. I swim laps, play tennis, lift weights, and ride a bicycle.

   c. I swim laps, play tennis, I lift weights, and bicycle riding is a change.

   d. swimming laps, tennis, lifting weights, and the bicycle.

   e. swim laps, play tennis, lifting weights, and riding a bicycle.

186. We all arrived at the theater on time, but before we bought our tickets, Candace <u>says that she's changed her mind and doesn't</u> want to see the movie after all.

   a. says that she's changed her mind and doesn't

   b. said that she had changed her mind and didn't

   c. is saying that she'd changed her mind and doesn't

   d. told us that she is changing her mind and didn't

   e. tells us that she had changed her mind and doesn't

187. State Senator Partridge wished <u>to insure the people that their tax dollars would be spent wisely.</u>

   a. to insure the people that their tax dollars would be spent wisely.

   b. that the people would be insured of tax dollars wisely spent.

   c. in assuring the people, that their tax dollars would be wisely spent.

   d. to assure the people that he would spend their tax dollars wisely..

   e. to assure and promise the people of his intentions to spend their tax dollars wisely.

188. Because he was given a local anesthetic, <u>Josh was conscience throughout the operation.</u>

   a. Josh was conscience throughout the operation.

   b. Josh had a conscience during the operation.

   c. the operation was completed with Josh consciousness.

   d. the operation was done while Josh held consciousness.

   e. Josh remained conscious throughout the operation.

SET 17 (Answers begin on page 129.)
Find the sentence that has a mistake in grammar or usage. If you find no mistakes, mark choice **d**.

189. a. Yes, it's true.
    b. The rain fell, and the river risen.
    c. My mother is a physician's assistant.
    d. No mistakes.

190. a. We searched every inch of the room.
    b. The words in this document does not make sense.
    c. We always have chicken for Sunday dinner.
    d. No mistakes.

191. a. It's going to be a long day.
    b. Derrick should of been here hours ago.
    c. Where are my golf clubs?
    d. No mistakes.

192. a. Reena took little Sean to kindergarten.
    b. Gregory is learning to be a chef.
    c. Paul drunk four bottles of grape soda.
    d. No mistakes.

193. a. Here are four different varieties of the same species.
    b. The oldest one of these books are not for sale.
    c. This is the most exciting vacation I have ever had.
    d. No mistakes.

194. a. When I go to the mall, I took Harrison with me.
    b. There are two buildings on this property.
    c. I was invited, but I declined the invitation.
    d. No mistakes.

195. a. David and Mickey danced in the street.
    b. Here is the photographs I wanted to show you.
    c. My grandfather owns a 1967 Mustang.
    d. No mistakes.

196. a. It has not rained since last April.
    b. The jurors walked solemnly into the room.
    c. Had we known, we would not have come.
    d. No mistakes.

197. a. The dog's barking woke us.
    b. Ursula has broke one of your plates.
    c. The sun rose from behind the mountain.
    d. No mistakes.

198. a. After we sat down to eat dinner, the phone rung.
    b. "Keep a positive attitude," he always says.
    c. Sign here.
    d. No mistakes.

199. a. The children's books are over there.
    b. She missed the bus and arrives late.
    c. There is hardly enough food for a mouse.
    d. No mistakes.

200. a. The winners were announced yesterday.
    b. Liam is the only one of the boys who were chosen.
    c. Although Nick was not selected, he was happy for the others.
    d. No mistakes.

201. a. He shook the crumbs from the tablecloth.
    b. We will strive to do our best.
    c. I see that Fred has wore his old shoes.
    d. No mistakes.

202. a. When I heard the alarm, I jump out of bed.
   b. Mr. Fox is the president of his own company.
   c. At night, I listened to jazz on the radio.
   d. No mistakes.

SET 18 (Answers begin on page 129.)
Choose the sentence that is the most clearly written and has the best construction.

203. a. All the children got out their rugs and took a nap.
   b. All the children have gotten out their rugs and took a nap.
   c. All the children got out their rugs and have taken a nap.
   d. All the children gotten out their rugs and taken a nap.

204. a. At first I was liking the sound of the wind, but later it got on my nerves.
   b. At first I liked the sound of the wind, but later it has gotten on my nerves.
   c. At first I like the sound of the wind, but later it got on my nerves.
   d. At first I liked the sound of the wind, but later it got on my nerves.

205. a. I became ill from eating too many fried clams.
   b. I became ill from eaten too many fried clams.
   c. I ate too many fried clams and becoming ill.
   d. I ate too many fried clams and become ill.

206. a. As the old saying goes, a cat may look at a king.
   b. A cat looking at a king, according to the old saying.
   c. The old saying being, a cat may look at a king.
   d. A cat looking at a king, in the old saying.

207. a. A longer happier life, caused by one's owning a pet.
   b. Owning a pet, for one to live a longer, happier life.
   c. To live a longer, happier life by one's owning a pet.
   d. Owning a pet can help one live a longer, happier life.

208. a. One of the first modern detectives in literature were created by Edgar Allan Poe.
   b. One of the first modern detectives in literature was created by Edgar Allan Poe.
   c. Edgar Allan Poe having created one of the first modern detectives in literature.
   d. In literature, one of the first modern detectives, created by Edgar Allan Poe.

209. a. My brother and I going to see the ball game.
   b. My brother and I are going to see the ball game.
   c. My brother and I seeing the ball game.
   d. My brother and I to the ball game.

210. a. I don't like fish as well as my sister does.
   b. I don't like fish as well as my sister.
   c. Fish isn't liked by me as well as my sister.
   d. My sister likes it, but I don't like fish as well.

211. a. After renting him the room, Alvin discovered Mr. Morris owned a cat.
b. After renting him the room, a cat was discovered to belong to Mr. Morris.
c. A cat belonging to Mr. Morris was discovered by Alvin after renting him a room.
d. After renting him a room, Mr. Morris was discovered by Alvin to own a cat.

212. a. We ate the popcorn and watch the movie.
b. While watching the movie, the popcorn was eaten.
c. Popcorn, while watching the movie, was eaten.
d. We ate the popcorn while we watched the movie.

SET 19 (Answers begin on page 130.)
For the following questions, choose the underlined part of the sentence that contains a grammatical error. If there are no errors, choose answer **e**.

213. All <u>employees</u> with two <u>years'</u> experience <u>are entitled</u> to full <u>benefits</u>, including health insurance, life
         a   b   c   d

insurance, a retirement plan, and stock options. <u>No error.</u>
                                   e

214. Because <u>their</u> afraid of air travel, my <u>mother</u> and my <u>Aunt Felicia</u> have decided to take the train
         a   b   c

<u>from Chicago to</u> New Orleans. <u>No error.</u>
     d   e

215. <u>To find</u> the perimeter of a <u>polygon, add</u> the <u>lengths</u> of <u>it's</u> sides. <u>No error.</u>
    a   b   c   d   e

216. After the <u>director and assistant</u> director both <u>resigned, we</u> all wondered <u>who would</u> be appointed
            a   b   c

<u>to fill</u> their positions. <u>No error.</u>
   d   e

217. Last spring, my <u>cousin and I</u> packed <u>the tent, the</u> sleeping <u>bags, and</u> a cooler filled with food and headed
                 a   b   c

<u>west.</u> <u>No error.</u>
 d   e

218. Although <u>it</u> usually has a soft <u>body and</u> muscular <u>feet</u>, some mollusks also <u>have</u> hard shells. <u>No error.</u>
          a   b   c   d   e

219. For all of those people <u>who have vowed</u> to give up fatty foods, video games, and shopping for the new
                                    a

year, <u>here's</u> an incentive to keep <u>him</u> on the <u>straight and</u> narrow path. <u>No error.</u>
      b   c   d   e

220. <u>Even as</u> the mainstream music industry pushes <u>further into</u> the digital world of solid state circuitry,
        a   b

<u>there is</u> a renewed interest in old-style <u>amplifiers and</u> speakers. <u>No error.</u>
   c   d   e

221. <u>To formalize</u> and commit <u>themselves</u> to <u>there</u> new government, the Pilgrims <u>signed</u> the Mayflower Pact.
        a   b   c   d

<u>No error.</u>
   e

222. Last summer around the <u>end of July,</u> my <u>brother,</u> my Aunt Clarissa, and <u>me</u> jumped into the Ford
                              a   b   c

<u>station wagon and</u> headed out of the city. <u>No error..</u>
   d   e

223. The term "blood type" <u>refers to</u> one of many groups <u>into which</u> a <u>person's</u> blood <u>can be categorized,</u>
                              a   b   c   d

based on the presence or absence of specific antigens. <u>No error.</u>
                                                        e

224. As you use <u>them,</u> remember that this glossary <u>is intended to be</u> a guide and that <u>nothing</u> in it is
                  a   b   c

is <u>absolute.</u> <u>No error.</u>
   d   e

225. Although chances of <u>being victimized</u> are slim, if <u>your</u> not careful, airport thieves—<u>who</u> look like
                          a   b   c

<u>ordinary travelers</u>—can make off with your purse, your wallet, your phone card, and all your credit
   d

cards. <u>No error.</u>
        e

226. The distinct geology of Cape Cod <u>began to form</u> about 20,000 years ago when the Wisconsin Glacier,
                                        a

up to two miles thick, pushed <u>its</u> way <u>south</u> from Canada, <u>stopped, and then</u> slowly receded. <u>No error.</u>
                              b   c   d   e

227. <u>Although</u> this <u>was</u> an <u>unusually dry</u> summer, the corn crop was not <u>seriously</u> damaged. <u>No error.</u>
        a   b   c   d   e

SET 20 (Answers begin on page 130.)
Fill in the blank with the correct pronoun.

228. That fine circus elephant now belongs to my
sister and _____.
a. I
b. me
c. mine
d. myself

229. The person _____ made these delicious
candied figs has my vote.
a. that
b. whom
c. who
d. whose

230. If you don't stop playing _____ video
games, you will miss the bus.
a. that
b. those
c. them
d. this

231. George and Michael left _____ backpacks
at school.
a. his
b. their
c. there
d. its

232. If you steal _____ artichoke from Petra's
garden, you'll be sorry.
a. them
b. those
c. that
d. these

233. We arranged the flowers and placed _____
in the center of the table.
a. it
b. this
c. them
d. that

234. _____ met more than ten years ago at a
mutual friend's birthday party.
a. Her and I
b. Her and me
c. She and me
d. She and I

235. My parents approved of _____ taking
guitar lessons.
a. my
b. me
c. I
d. mine

SET 21 (Answers begin on page 131.)
Replace the underlined words with the phrase that
best completes the sentence. If the sentence is correct
as is, choose **a**.

236. It was either Kendra or Zoë who <u>brought their</u>
volleyball to the picnic.
a. brought their
b. brought her
c. brought their
d. brang their
e. brang her

237. <u>Whose car will you take when you drive to</u> <u>their</u> house?

    a.   Whose car will you take when you drive to their

    b.   Whose car will you take when you drive to there

    c.   Who's car will you take when you drive to their

    d.   Who's car will take when you drive to there

    e.   Which car will you take when you drive to there

238. <u>If someone is looking</u> for the best car loan, you should compare interest rates at several banks.

    a.   If someone is looking

    b.   When one is looking

    c.   If you are looking

    d.   To have a person look

    e.   When someone is about to look

239. <u>When two angles have the same degree</u> <u>measure, it is said to be congruent.</u>

    a.   When two angles have the same degree measure, it is said to be congruent.

    b.   When two angles has the same degree measure, it is said to be congruent.

    c.   Two angles with the same degree measure is said to be congruent.

    d.   They are congruent when the said two angles has the same degree measure.

    e.   When two angles have the same degree measure, they are said to be congruent.

240. <u>The friendship between Andre and Robert</u> <u>began when he and his</u> family moved to Ohio.

    a.   The friendship between Andre and Robert began when he and his

    b.   Andre and Robert's friendship began when he and his

    c.   The friendship among the two boys began when he and his

    d.   The friendship between Andre and Robert began when Robert and his

    e.   Andre and Robert's friendship began when their

SET 22 (Answers begin on page 131.)

Find the sentence that has a mistake in grammar or usage. If you find no mistakes, mark choice **d.**

241. a. Of the four of us, I am the tallest.

      b. Wilson's brother is a chemical engineer.

      c. That fine circus elephant now belongs to my sister and I.

      d. No mistakes.

242. a. Help is on the way.

      b. The firemen used a ladder to reach the kitten.

      c. Don't slip on the icy sidewalk.

      d. No mistakes.

243. a. His family has lived in this town for thirty-five years.

      b. You're the only one who can remember that song.

      c. That's the quickest way to get to Sylvia's house.

      d. No mistakes.

244. a. "Meet me at six o'clock," she said.
  b. Tired of running, she slowed her pace to a fast walk.
  c. Gabriel and me will attend the geography bee.
  d. No mistakes.

245. a. Sheila's sister wanted to accompany us to the party.
  b. Who's scarf is this?
  c. "Be sure to wear something comfortable," she said.
  d. No mistakes.

246. a. The main problem Jim had was too many parking tickets.
  b. As the bears ran toward us, it was growling.
  c. Try using less butter next time.
  d. No mistakes.

247. a. Kamala was the most intelligent person in the group.
  b. The Eiffel Tower is in Paris, France.
  c. Nick Carraway is a character in *The Great Gatsby*.
  d. No mistakes.

248. a. They weren't the only ones who didn't like the movie.
  b. "Please come back another time," Aunt Julie begged.
  c. "Threes a crowd," he always says.
  d. No mistakes.

249. a. The first house on the street is there's.
  b. I love the fireworks on the Fourth of July.
  c. My grandparents live in San Juan, Puerto Rico.
  d. No mistakes.

250. a. Either Cassie nor I heard the door open.
  b. How many people signed the Declaration of Independence?
  c. Draw up a plan before you make your decision.
  d. No mistakes.

251. a. It's not my fault that you and him got caught.
  b. "Do you brush twice a day?" Dr. Evans asked.
  c. What's the weather report?
  d. No mistakes.

252. a. Couldn't you arrive fashionably late?
  b. You're assumption is correct.
  c. I know that Bowser will be well treated.
  d. No mistakes.

253. a. We invited Mayor Chen to speak at our school.
  b. The alarm sounded, and the firefighters jumped into the truck.
  c. The committee members should work as hard as one can.
  d. No mistakes.

254. a. He wore two different shoes to class.
  b. Rhonda's sister bought a new Pontiac.
  c. Lake Superior is the largest of the Great Lakes.
  d. No mistakes.

255. a. She and I have been friends for more than ten years.
  b. Is that one of the O'Farrell children?
  c. They took too much time to answer.
  d. No mistakes.

SET 23 (Answers begin on page 131.)
Choose the sentence that is the most clearly written and has the best construction.

256. a. Officer DeAngelo phoned his partner every day when he was in the hospital.
    b. When his partner was in the hospital, Officer DeAngelo phoned him every day.
    c. When in the hospital, a phone call was made every day by Officer DeAngelo to his partner.
    d. His partner received a phone call from Officer DeAngelo every day while he was in the hospital.

257. a. Some of the case transcripts I have to type are very long, but that doesn't bother one if the cases are interesting.
    b. Some of the case transcripts I have to type are very long, but that doesn't bother you if the cases are interesting.
    c. Some of the case transcripts I have to type are very long, but it doesn't bother a person if the cases are interesting.
    d. Some of the case transcripts I have to type are very long, but that doesn't bother me if the cases are interesting.

258. a. In search of the missing teenagers, who still had not been found through snake-ridden underbrush all day, the exhausted volunteers had struggled.
    b. All day the exhausted volunteers had struggled through snake-ridden underbrush in search of the missing teenagers, who still had not been found.
    c. All day the exhausted volunteers had struggled through snake-ridden underbrush who still had not been found in searching for the missing teenagers.
    d. The exhausted volunteers who still had not found in search of the missing teenagers when they had struggled through snake-ridden underbrush.

259. a. One New York publisher have estimated that 50,000 to 60,000 people in the United States want an anthology that includes the complete works of William Shakespeare.
    b. One New York publisher has estimated that 50,000 to 60,000 people in the United States want a anthology that includes the complete works of William Shakespeare.
    c. One New York publisher has estimated that 50,000 to 60,000 people in the United States want an anthology that includes the complete works of William Shakespeare.
    d. One New York publisher has estimated that 50,000 to 60,000 people in the United States want an anthology that included the complete works of William Shakespeare.

S·E·C·T·I·O·N 4

MODIFIERS

Adjectives and adverbs modify subjects and/or their actions in a sentence. In the sentence, "The orange and striped cat leapt nimbly across the dresser," adjectives and adverbs specify what kind of cat (an "orange and striped cat") and how that cat leapt ("nimbly"). All too often adjectives and adverbs are confused for one another. However, in this section you will put each in its proper place and in its proper form.

First, you have to know the definition of a modifier:

✓ A **modifier** describes or limits another word.→*Lily* is a subject. Add the word *tiger* before lily and the subject is modified: It is now a specific type of lily. *Pushed* is an action word. Add *shyly* and the action is limited: It is now a gentler action. Put the subject, its action and the modifiers all together and the sentence reads: *Unlike its fierce namesake, the tiger lily pushed its head shyly through the soil.*

TYPES OF MODIFIERS

✓ **Adjectives** modify nouns or pronouns. (*Hint:* An *adjective* answers one of three questions: which one, what kind, or how many?)
✓ **Adverbs** modify verbs, adjectives, other adverbs, or whole groups of words. (*Hint:* An adverb answers one of four questions: where, when, how, or to what extent?)
✓ **Comparatives** are adjectives and adverbs used to compare two things.

✓ **Superlatives** are adjectives and adverbs used to compare more than two things.

Follow this guideline and you will do well (*well* describes the verb *to do*; therefore it is an adverb!):

✓ Always identify whether a modifier describes or limits a sentence's subject or its action.

✓ Use *good* and *bad* to describe nouns.

✓ Use *well* and *badly* to describe verbs, except when *well* means "fit" or "healthy." When *well* describes a state of being, it is an adjective.➞*With repetition, you will soon write well. Well* describes how the subject writes; it is an adverb. *After two months of physical therapy, Bob was well. Well* describes Bob's state of being; it is an adjective.

✓ Use an adjective after a *linking verb*. The following words are linking verbs when they express a state of being: look, sound, smell, feel, taste, appear, seem, become, grow, turn, prove, remain and stay. ➞*Howard leaned over and surreptitiously smelled Lee; she smelled sweet. Surreptitiously* describes how Howard sniffed at the other person; in this case, it is an adverb because it describes the act of smelling. *Sweet* describes Lee; the word smell links the adjective back to the subject.

✓ Use the adjective *fewer* to describe plural nouns and the adjective *less* to describe singular nouns.

✓ Use the word *number* to describe plural nouns and the word *amount* to describe singular nouns.

✓ Add *-er* to a modifier or place the word *more* or *less* before the modifier to compare two things. This creates a comparison. (*Hint*: One to two syllable modifiers usually receive the suffix *-er*; modifiers with more than two syllables use *more* or *less* before them.)

✓ Add *-est* to a modifier or place the word *most* or *least* before the modifier to indicate the extreme degree of a thing (*Hint*: One to two syllable modifiers receive *-est*; modifiers with more than two syllables use *most* or *least* before them.)

✓ Avoid double comparatives or double superlatives. Adding the suffix -er or -est to a modifier and preceding the modifier with *more* or *most* is redundant. ➞*Lindsey amazed the class with her grammatical skills; she was the most smartest person they had ever seen. Lindsey* is already *the smartest. Most* also means smartest—the phrase *most smartest* is redundant.

✓ Avoid double negatives unless you mean to express the positive.➞*Tom hardly did not feel tense whenever he approached grammar. Hardly* and *did not* cancel each other out. The sentence really reads: Tom felt tense whenever approaching grammar.

✓ Avoid illogical comparisons. Some words already indicate an extreme degree; like double comparatives and double superlatives, adding the word *more* or *most* before such words is redundant. ➞*Some women believe Brad Pitt is more perfect than Matt Damon.* There are not degrees of perfection; one is either perfect or not perfect. However, one can more nearly approach perfection than someone else.

SET 24 (Answers begin on page 132.)

For the following questions, choose the underlined part of the sentence that contains a grammatical error. If there are no errors, choose answer **e.**

260. <u>Frightened,</u> the little boy screamed <u>loud</u> as his <u>neighbor's</u> friendly <u>eighty-pound dog</u> bounded up the
     a   b   c   d

sidewalk. <u>No error.</u>
       e

261. Ian Anderson—<u>once the leader</u> of the 1970s rock group Jethro Tull and now a fish farmer in Great
              a

Britain—<u>has</u> about 400 employees and <u>produces</u> about 20 million <u>pounds</u> of smoked salmon each year.
      b   c   d

<u>No error.</u>
   e

262. Of the three girls <u>who</u> have <u>recently joined</u> the basketball <u>team</u>, Frieda is the <u>taller.</u> <u>No error.</u>
            a   b   c   d   e

263. At about 4,000 miles long, the Yangtze, a <u>major</u> east-west trade and <u>transportation route</u>, is <u>easily</u> the
                           a   b   c

<u>longest</u> river in China and in Asia. <u>No error.</u>
  d   e

264. Despite its daunting <u>three-hour</u> length, the <u>movie's</u> popularity <u>continues to grow;</u> last week <u>it took</u> in
                a   b   c   d

12.7 million dollars. <u>No error.</u>
            e

265. The love seat is now <u>being installed</u> in some New York movie theaters, <u>giving</u> couples the option of
             a   b

lifting the arm <u>between</u> the seats to create a <u>more cozier</u> viewing experience. <u>No error.</u>
         c   d   e

266. Some buildings, <u>such as</u> the White House, Saint Paul's <u>Cathedral,</u> and the Taj Mahal, deserve to be
           a   b

preserved not only because of <u>their</u> artistic excellence <u>but also</u> because of their symbolic associations.
                  c   d

<u>No error.</u>
   e

267. Because they <u>close</u> resemble sound arguments, fallacious arguments can sound convincing, so be sure to
            a   b

     <u>carefully organize</u> your thoughts when <u>you're</u> writing an opinion paper <u>No error</u>.
          c   d   e

268. In this cookbook, <u>you'll discover</u> colorful, easy to <u>prepare, and</u> great-tasting recipes <u>for even</u> your <u>more</u>
                      a   b   c   d

     diet-conscious guests. <u>No error.</u>
                      e

269. <u>When</u> the professor called out his name, <u>he walked</u> rather <u>hesitant</u> to the front of the room and stood
     a   b   c

     <u>there</u> shaking. <u>No error.</u>
      d   e

270. The puppy had been treated <u>bad</u> by <u>its</u> previous <u>owner, but</u> the people at the animal shelter <u>worked hard</u>
                           a   b   c   d

     to find a loving home for little Scotty. <u>No error.</u>
                                   e

SET 25 (Answers begin on page 132.)
Fill in the blank with the correct adjective or adverb.

271. In many popular movies today, the heroes are
_____ armed than the villains.
  a. more heavily
  b. more heavy
  c. heavier
  d. more heavier

272. The cake I made last week tasted _____
than the one I made today.
  a. best
  b. more better
  c. better
  d. more good

273. After winning the yo-yo contest, Lydia skipped
_____ down the street.
  a. happy
  b. happiest
  c. more happily
  d. happily

274. Of the three brothers, Andre is the _____.
  a. taller
  b. tallest
  c. more tall
  d. most tallest

275. Riding the Tornado at the amusement park
was _____ than I thought it would be.
  a. more terrifying
  b. more terrifyingly
  c. terrifying
  d. most terrifying

276. This year our company sold _____ magazine subscriptions than ever before.
- a. less
- b. lesser
- c. few
- d. fewer

SET 26 (Answers begin on page 133.)
Replace the underlined words with the word or phrase that is grammatically correct. If the sentence is correct as is, choose answer **a**.

277. The book had <u>a frighteningly and unhappy ending</u>.
- a. a frighteningly and unhappy ending.
- b. a frighteningly and unhappily ending.
- c. an ending that was frightening and unhappily.
- d. a frightening and unhappy ending.
- e. an ending that was frightening and it was also an unhappy one.

278. Since his release from jail in 1990, Nelson Mandela has emerged <u>as the more prominent</u> spokesperson for South Africa's anti-apartheid movement.
- a. as the more prominent
- b. as the most prominent
- c. as the most prominently
- d. as the more prominently
- e. like the most prominent

279. Surprisingly, my younger sister dresses <u>more conservatively than I do.</u>
- a. more conservatively than I do.
- b. more conservative than I do.
- c. more conservative than me.
- d. more conservatively than me.
- e. the most conservative in opposition to me.

280. <u>There wasn't nothing that could have been easier.</u>
- a. There wasn't nothing that could have been easier.
- b. There was nothing that could have been more easier.
- c. Nothing could have been more easier.
- d. Nothing couldn't have been more easy.
- e. Nothing could have been easier.

281. <u>I was clearly the happiest person in the crowd.</u>
- a. I was clearly the happiest person in the crowd.
- b. It was clear that I was the happier person in the crowd.
- c. Of all the people in the crowd, I was clearly the happier.
- d. In the crowd, clearly, I was the happier person.
- e. Of all the people in the crowd, clearly, I being the happiest.

282. Our team scored <u>less baskets today than we did</u> last Tuesday.
- a. less baskets today than we did
- b. today less baskets than were scored
- c. fewer baskets today then on
- d. fewer baskets today than we did
- e. a lesser number of baskets today then we did

283. Strip mining, the <u>cheaper</u> method of mining, is controversial because it jeopardizes the environment.
- a. cheaper
- b. more cheap
- c. most cheapest
- d. cheapest
- e. more cheaply

SET 27 (Answers begin on page 133.)
Find the sentence that has a mistake in grammar or usage. If you find no mistakes, mark choice **d.**

284. a. The steam rose up from the hot pavement.
   b. She put the kitten down carefully beside its mom.
   c. Neither of us is going to the party.
   d. No mistakes.

285. a. The lost dog wandered sad through the streets.
   b. Frustrated, Boris threw his pencil across the room.
   c. We'll stop at their house first.
   d. No mistakes.

286. a. I don't want to participate no longer.
   b. If you're not sure, look in the dictionary.
   c. "I will try to do better," Lauren promised.
   d. No mistakes.

287. a. Have you ever read the book *Little House on the Prairie*?
   b. She urged me not to go.
   c. Stop, look, and listen.
   d. No mistakes.

288. a. Anne will head out first, and Nick will follow her.
   b. Maya Angelou, a famous poet, has recently directed a movie.
   c. The clerk asked for my address and phone number.
   d. No mistakes.

289. a. We sold less cookies this year than we did last year.
   b. That parrot doesn't talk.
   c. Don't spend too much money.
   d. No mistakes.

290. a. She spread the frosting too thickly.
   b. "What is your answer?" she asked.
   c. We waited while he stopped to make a phone call.
   d. No mistakes.

291. a. Between the three of us, we should find the answer.
   b. Alberto laughed loudly when he saw us.
   c. They're looking for another apartment.
   d. No mistakes.

292. a. The Adirondacks are mountains in New York.
   b. President Carter gave the Panama Canal back to Panama.
   c. That river is terribly polluted.
   d. No mistakes.

293. a. *Trading Spaces* is probably the most daring show on television.
   b. Which color do you like better, the teal or the flamigo pink?
   c. Mango-peach berry juice is the most awfulest drink.
   d. No mistakes.

S·E·C·T·I·O·N 5

PARAGRAPH DEVELOPMENT

Paragraphs are groups of related sentences that form complete units. They usually support the main ideas of an essay, article, or story; however, every paragraph has an identity and an idea of its own. A paragraph is like a miniature essay. For practice in paragraph development and unity, Section 5 will ask you to identify the best topic sentence for a particular paragraph, to find the sentence that best develops a topic, and to eliminate the sentence that does not belong. You will also choose the best order for a group of sentences. The guideline below will help you organize your paragraphs. Since paragraphs and essays are similar in structure, these guidelines can be applied to the organization of an entire essay.

✓ Write a paragraph to explore a single idea using a **topic sentence** near the beginning of the paragraph.

✓ Maintain **paragraph unity**, the logical development of a single idea in a group of related sentences, by using:

- a **consistent organizing strategy**. Paragraphs not only present ideas, they group detailed information necessary to develop ideas. Organizing strategies arrange that information into logical and easy-to-anticipate patterns. These patterns can be top-to-bottom, left-to-right, near-to-far, then-to-now, beginning-to-ending, general-to-specific, least important-to-most important, least familiar-to-most familiar or simplest-to-most complex. Other strategies use stories, descriptions, examples, definitions, categorizations, comparisons and contrasts, or causes and effects to logically organize information. As you become more proficient at writing, you will probably incorporate more than one strategy in a paragraph.

- **parallelisms.** By arranging sentences in identical patterns, a writer can convey that two different things are equally important. Patterning sentence structure is called parallelism.➞*Bob quickly ran to the store; Alex also quickly ran to the store. It was a race to see who was fastest.*

- **repeated words or word groups.** Though similar to parallelisms, repeated word groups can occur anywhere in a sentence.➞*Humans **still** worship trees. Rain or shine, they **still** marvel at the solstice.*

- **transitional phrases or words** to connect sentences and/or ideas➞ *First*, Katie gathered the ingredients. **Then** she assembled the meal.

✓ **Important:** Try not to shift the number of things, a pronoun's case or a verb's tense in a paragraph unless your organizing strategy requires it.

SET 28 (Answers begin on page 134.)
For each of the following paragraphs, choose the topic sentence that best fits the rest of the paragraph.

_____. Residents have been directed to use the new plastic bins as their primary recycling containers. These new containers will make picking up recyclables faster and easier.

294. a. The city has distributed standardized recycling containers to all households.
   b. Recycling has become a way of life for most people.
   c. While most Americans recycle, they also use more resources than residents of other countries.
   d. Even small cities have begun recycling to pick up used glass, plastic, and paper.

_____. Telecommuters produce, on average, 20% more than if they were to work in an office. Their flexible schedule allows them to balance both their family and work responsibilities.

295. a. People who work in offices make up a large part of the U.S. work force.
   b. Office workers who telecommute from their own homes are more productive and have greater flexibility.
   c. Many companies now offer their employees benefits that were not available just a few years ago.
   d. One of the biggest problems in corporate America is the lack of skilled office workers.

_____. No search of a person's home or personal effects may be conducted without a written search warrant. This means that a judge must justify a search before it can be conducted.

296. a. There is an old saying that a person's home is his or her castle.
b. Much of the U.S. legal system was based on the old British system.
c. The Fourth Amendment to the Constitution protects citizens against unreasonable searches.
d. "Personal effects" is a term that refers to the belongings of a person.

_____. You must imitate as closely as possible the parents' methods of feeding. First, hold the beak open using thumb and forefinger. Then, introduce food into the beak with tweezers or an eye-dropper.

297. a. Recently, I read an article about baby birds.
b. Hand-rearing wounded or orphaned baby birds requires skill.
c. Baby birds are very special creatures, and they are also very small.
d. I have been told that you should not touch a baby bird that has fallen out of its nest.

_____. All waves, though, have common characteristics that govern their height. The height of a wave is determined by its speed, the distance it travels, and the length of time the wind blows.

298. a. Currents, unlike waves, are caused by steady winds or temperature fluctuations.
b. Tsunamis used to be called tidal waves.
c. Ocean waves can vary from tiny ripples to powerful, raging swells.
d. A breaker is when a wave gets top-heavy and tips over.

_____. When people respect the law too much, they will follow it blindly. They will say that the majority has decided on this law and therefore I must obey it. They will not stop to consider whether or not the law is fair.

299. a. Some people say there is too little respect for the law, but I say there is too much respect for it.
b. Sometimes a judge will decide that a law is unfair.
c. I believe that the majority of the people in this country do not understand what it means to have respect for other people.
d. Most of the laws passed at the end of the twentieth century are fair laws.

Gary is a very distinguished looking man with a touch of gray at the temples. Even in his early fifties, he is still the one to turn heads. He enjoys spending most of his time admiring his profile in the mirror. In fact, he considers his good looks to be his second most important asset in the world. The first, however, is money. He is lucky in this area, too, having been born into a wealthy family. _____. He loved the power his wealth had given him. He could buy whatever he desired, be that people, places, or things. Gary checked that mirror often and felt great delight with what he saw.

300. a. Gary's gray hair was his worst characteristic.
b. Conceit was the beginning and the end of Gary's character; conceit of person and situation.
c. Gary felt blessed to be wealthy and the joy consumed his every thought.
d. The only objects of Gary's respect were others who held positions in society.

The term "spices" is a pleasant one, whether it connotes fine French cuisine or a down-home, cinnamon-flavored apple pie. _____. Individuals have traveled the world seeking exotic spices for profit and, in searching, have changed the course of history. Indeed, to gain control of lands harboring new spices, nations have actually gone to war.

301. a. The taste and aroma of spices are the main elements that make food such a source of fascination and pleasure.
b. The term might equally bring to mind Indian curry made thousands of miles away and those delicious barbecued ribs sold down on the corner.
c. It is exciting to find a good cookbook and experiment with spices from other lands—indeed, it is one way to travel around the globe!
d. The history of spices, however, is another matter altogether, often exciting, at times filled with danger and intrigue.

_____. Although these mechanical alarms are fairly recent, the idea of a security system is not new. The oldest alarm system was probably a few strategically placed dogs that discouraged intruders with a loud warning cry.

302. a. Anyone who lives in a large, modern city has heard the familiar sound of electronic security alarms.
b. Everyone knows that a large, barking dog will scare away strangers, even the mail carrier.
c. Why spend money on an alarm system when you can get the same service from an animal?
d. Without a good alarm system, your place of business could be vandalized.

_____. According to scholars, these patterns almost certainly represent the labyrinth that held the Minotaur, a monster with the head of a bull and the body of a man. Legend has it that, in ancient times, King Minos built the labyrinth in order to imprison the Minotaur, which loved to dine on human flesh.

303. a. Patterned corridors are commonplace in many architectural structures.
   b. In the palace at Knossos, on the isle of Crete, there is a corridor leading to the outside that is decorated with coils and spiral patterns.
   c. Archeologists contend that patterns on the walls and corridors of ancient architectural structures are usually meaningful.
   d. Scholars who have studied the palace at Knossos, on the isle of Crete, are at a loss to explain the meaning of the coils and spirals on its corridor walls.

_____. It is important to take special precautions to keep these medications in a secure place, where a child cannot get to them. Every item in the medicine cabinet should be labeled in large letters and attached to the container. Even if you believe the medicine cabinet is too high for a child to reach, it should be locked at all times.

304. a. Many families have small children.
   b. Many medications are extremely dangerous if swallowed.
   c. If your child accidentally swallows a medicine, rush him or her to the hospital right away!
   d. New, life-saving medicines are being approved by the FDA every day.

_____. It is true that Ernest Hemingway went to war to gather material for his stories, and F. Scott Fitzgerald lived a life of dissolution that destroyed him. However, Emily Brontë seldom ventured outside her father's tiny country rectory, yet she wrote _Wuthering Heights_, a tale of passionate love and intense hatred, and one of the greatest works in the English language.

305. a. It is not necessary for a writer to endanger his or her life in order to have something to write about.
   b. There are many ways for gifted writers to collect material for their stories and novels.
   c. Ernest Hemingway, F. Scott Fitzgerald, and Emily Brontë are all known for the passion with which their work is imbued.
   d. Hemingway and Fitzgerald are well-known for their reckless lifestyles, which nevertheless gave rise to some of the finest works in the English language.

_____. Hearsay that depends on the statement's truthfulness is inadmissible because the witness does not appear in court and swear an oath to tell the truth. This means that his or her demeanor when making the statement is not visible to the jury, the accuracy of the statement cannot be tested under cross-examination, and to introduce it would be to deprive the accused of the constitutional right to confront the accuser.

306. a. Hearsay evidence is not acceptable in a criminal trial because the witness cannot be cross-examined.

b. Hearsay evidence in a trial is inadmissible because there is too great a chance that it will be false.

c. The definition of hearsay evidence is the "secondhand reporting of a statement" and is sometimes allowable.

d. Hearsay evidence, which is the secondhand reporting of a statement, is allowed in court only when the truth of the statement is irrelevant.

_____. Any truck that finishes its assigned route before the end of the workers' shift will return to the sanitation lot, where supervisors will provide materials for workers to use in cleaning off the graffiti. Because the length of time it takes to complete different routes varies, trucks will no longer be assigned to a specific route but will be rotated among the routes. Therefore, workers should no longer leave personal items in the trucks, as they will

not necessarily be using the same truck each day as they did in the past.

307. a. Graffiti on city trucks is unsightly and gives city residents a poor impression of the Sanitation Department.

b. The Sanitation Department greatly appreciates city workers' extra efforts in cleaning graffiti off the city trucks.

c. Beginning next month, the Sanitation Department will institute a program intended to remove the graffiti from sanitation trucks.

d. City workers should keep a sharp lookout for persons spray-painting graffiti on Sanitation Department trucks.

_____. One type of tickler system is the index-card file with 12 large dividers, one for each month, and 31 small dividers, one for each day. Whenever secretaries need to schedule a reminder, they jot it down on a card and place it behind the appropriate divider. Each morning, they review the reminders for that particular day.

308. a. As busy secretaries, we cannot expect to remember all the details of our daily responsibilities without some help.

b. At the beginning of the day, good secretaries review and organize the tasks they must attend to during that day.

c. The word "tickler" perfectly describes the organizational system to which it refers.

d. All secretaries need a good reminder system, sometimes known as a "tickler" system because it tickles the memory.

_____. Space shuttle astronauts, because they spend only about a week in space, undergo minimal wasting of bone and muscle. But when longer stays in microgravity or zero gravity are contemplated, as in the proposed space station or a two-year roundtrip voyage to Mars, these problems are of particular concern because they could become acute. Fortunately, studies show that muscle atrophy can be kept largely at bay with appropriate exercise. Unfortunately, bone loss caused by reduced gravity cannot.

309. a. Space flight, especially if it is prolonged, can be hazardous to the health of the astronauts.
b. The tissues of human beings are ill-prepared for the stresses placed upon them by space flight.
c. In space flight, astronauts must deal with two vexing physiological foes—muscle atrophy and bone loss.
d. Travel on the space shuttle does less damage to an astronaut's bones and muscles than an extended stay on a space station.

_____. Rather, asthma is now understood to be a chronic inflammatory disorder of the airways—that is, inflammation makes the airways chronically sensitive. When these hyper-responsive airways are irritated, air flow is limited, and attacks of coughing, wheezing, chest tightness, and difficulty breathing occur.

310. a. No longer is asthma considered a condition with isolated, acute episodes of bronchospasm.
b. The true nature of asthma has only recently been understood.
c. Since the true character of asthma is now understood, there is more hope for a cure than there was in earlier times.
d. No age is exempt from asthma, although it occurs most often in childhood and early adulthood.

_____. Many experts, including those in the American Diabetes Association, recommend that 50 to 60 percent of daily calories of patients suffering from non-insulin-dependent diabetes (NIDD) come from carbohydrates, 12 to 20 percent from protein, and no more than 30 percent from fat. Foods that are rich in carbohydrates, like breads, cereals, fruits, and vegetables, break down into glucose during digestion, causing blood glucose to rise. Additionally, studies have shown that cooked foods raise blood glucose higher than raw, unpeeled foods.

311. a. In 1986, a National Institute of Health panel gave broad recommendations as to the type of diet that is best for non-insulin-dependent diabetics.
b. It is extremely important for certain medical patients to watch what they eat.
c. A good cookbook is the best friend a non-insulin-dependent diabetes (NIDD) patient can have!
d. Non-insulin-dependent diabetes patients can lead long, healthy lives if only they pay attention to their diets.

SET 29 (Answers begin on page 135.)
Choose the answer that best develops the topic sentence given.

312. Indoor pollution sources that release gases or particles into the air are the primary cause of indoor air-quality problems in homes.
    a. Inadequate ventilation can increase indoor pollutant levels by not bringing in enough outdoor air to dilute emissions from indoor sources.
    b. Some physicians believe that the dangers of "environmental allergens" are greatly exaggerated.
    c. Although there are more potential pollution sources today than ever before, environmental activists are working hard to make our world a safer place.
    d. I'll choose a good, old-fashioned log cabin any day to the kind of squeaky-clean, hermetically-sealed modern condos you find in the big American cities.

313. In the Middle Ages, red hair was associated with evil, so to have red hair was to be in constant danger.
    a. People with red hair are sometimes singled out and called unflattering nicknames.
    b. The Middle Ages was a time of great turmoil and people were often summarily executed by being burned at the stake.
    c. During that time period, people with red hair were sometimes killed because they were thought to be witches.
    d. Red hair is passed on genetically from parent to child.

314. Because of the cost of medical care these days, many Americans self-diagnose and self-medicate.
    a. Because of the abundance of over-the-counter medications that exist, this can be a bewildering task.
    b. Today, much of the work doctors used to do is done by medical assistants, who are even allowed to write prescriptions.
    c. With so many prescriptions written by doctors each day, there is always the chance of dangerous drug interactions.
    d. Medical care today is routinely done by specialists, who are apt to be less personally involved than the old-style family doctor.

315. One of the most fascinating discoveries in modern physics is the idea that light can behave both as particles and as waves.
    a. In order to understand quantum physics one must know a great deal about mathematics.
    b. What is called "empty space" by laypersons is really not empty at all, but a sea of negative energy electrons.
    c. This idea, first suggested by the French noblemen Louis de Broglie, is counter-intuitive, but can be empirically proven.
    d. Some physicists say that nothing is real unless it is observed.

316. In spite of technological advances, much communication between companies and businesses is still done by regular mail, and office workers must face that fact.
  a. Every day the U.S. Post Office is subjected to a deluge of junk mail.
  b. Handling the boss's mail is often an important part of the secretary's job.
  c. It is hard to believe that a century ago the mail was delivered on horseback!
  d. A mailroom worker is sometimes promoted to a more responsible position.

317. There are lots of good reasons to work for the Immigration and Naturalization Service (INS): interesting and diverse work, good benefits, job security, and more.
  a. The INS inspects aliens to determine their admissibility for entry into the U.S.
  b. The INS is an agency of the United States Department of Justice.
  c. As an INS employee, you'll earn a respectable salary, even at the entry level.
  d. Before you are hired for an INS job, you may be subject to a background check.

318. It is a myth that financial aid for higher education just means getting a loan and going into heavy debt.
  a. It's important for young people to avoid starting out their working lives under a load of indebtedness.
  b. Financial aid is meant to help those students who could otherwise not attend college.
  c. The truth is that students in medicine and law are often able to pay back their student loans in short order.
  d. The fact is that most schools have their own grants and scholarships, which the student doesn't have to pay back, and a large percentage of students get these.

319. This contract will confirm our agreement in connection with your services as freelance writer for the work entitled *Why Kangaroos Can't Fly.*
  a. The title, although rather silly, accurately sums up the tone and style of the book.
  b. You agree to assist us in preparation of the book by developing content for it, based on your zoo-keeping experience.
  c. It is important to have a legal contract before turning your written work over to a publishing company.
  d. This book will make an important contribution to kangaroo lore around the world.

320. The continuing fascination of the public with movie star Marilyn Monroe is puzzling, yet it is still strong, even after four decades.
  a. Marilyn became a star in the 1950s. She died in 1962.
  b. The film that most clearly demonstrates her talent is *The Misfits.* She is also known for her role in *Some Like It Hot.*
  c. Her name was originally Norma Jean. However, she didn't like this name and changed it to Marilyn.
  d. One reason might be her quick rise to fame. Another reason, however, might simply be her life's sad and premature end.

321. Before we learn how to truly love someone else we must learn how to love the face in the mirror.

    a. Don't be shy about meeting members of the opposite sex.

    b. No one can really love you the way you can love yourself.

    c. Love is not something that lasts unless one is very lucky.

    d. Learning to accept ourselves for what we are will teach us how to accept another person.

322. During colonial times in America, juries were encouraged to ask questions of the parties in the courtroom.

    a. The jurors were, in fact, expected to investigate the facts of the case themselves. If jurors conducted an investigation today, we would throw out the case.

    b. Many states are experimenting with new ways to get more people to serve on juries. All eligible voters can be called to serve.

    c. There are usually two attorneys: a prosecutor and a defense attorney. This sometimes makes the courtroom lively.

    d. There were thirteen colonies. Each colony at first had its own legal system.

323. Many office professionals are interested in replacing the currently used keyboard, known as the QWERTY keyboard, with a keyboard that can make offices more efficient.

    a. Most middle-school students learn to type on a keyboard using the QWERTY system. This system has been in use for years.

    b. The rate at which a person can type is usually faster on a computer keyboard than it is on a typewriter. There are studies that indicate this.

    c. The best choice is the Dvorak keyboard. Studies have shown that people using the Dvorak keyboard can type 20 to 30 percent faster.

    d. The currently used keyboard would appear to be a slower system. Many people, however, are reluctant to replace it.

324. Ginkgo biloba extract is the most commonly prescribed plant remedy in the world.

    a. There are many plant remedies, including the ones that can be purchased in health-food stores. Not all plant remedies have been approved.

    b. It is a highly refined compound produced from the leaves of the ginkgo tree. Many people take ginkgo to treat conditions such as headaches, asthma, and hearing loss.

    c. Gingko has also been widely prescribed in Europe. It has been approved by the German government for the treatment of memory loss.

    d. A 1977 study with gingko was conducted with twenty patients. These patients ranged in age from 62 to 85.

325. Life on Earth is ancient and, even at its first appearance, unimaginably complex.

  a. Scientists place its beginnings at some 3000 million years ago. This is when the first molecule floated up out of the ooze with the unique ability to replicate itself.

  b. The most complex life form is, of course, the mammal. The most complex mammal is us.

  c. It is unknown exactly where life started. It is unknown exactly where the first molecule was "born."

  d. Darwin's theory of evolution was an attempt to explain what essentially remains a great mystery. His theory, of course, has been discounted by some people.

SET 30 (Answers begin on page 136.)
For each of the following paragraphs, choose the sentence that does NOT belong.

(1) The cassowary, a solitary, meat-eating creature who makes its home deep in the jungles of New Guinea, hardly seems like a bird at all. (2) It is enormous, weighing up to 190 pounds. (3) Its plumage is more like hair than feathers; its song is a deep, menacing rumble; and it has lost the capability of flight. (4) Human beings have long been fascinated by birds, particularly by their ability to fly.

326.
  a. Sentence 1
  b. Sentence 2
  c. Sentence 3
  d. Sentence 4

(1) Story-telling should speak first to the heart and only second to the intellect. (2) It should, in Isaac Bashevis Singer's words, "be both clear and profound," and it should also entertain. (3) Many fine writing programs have sprung up across the United States. (4) The new writer should avoid creating pieces that are deliberately obscure and impossible to understand except by a small, elite group of other writers.

327.
  a. Sentence 1
  b. Sentence 2
  c. Sentence 3
  d. Sentence 4

(1) Almost everyone is familiar with the term online, but many people are puzzled as to exactly what it entails. (2) Every day, computers are dropping in price and becoming more affordable. (3) Getting online can be a frustrating experience, as one negotiates complex webs and nets of information. (4) Indeed, unless one has a good teacher or an excellent guidebook, one may become hopelessly lost in cyberspace!

328.
  a. Sentence 1
  b. Sentence 2
  c. Sentence 3
  d. Sentence 4

(1) Ratatouille is a dish that has grown in popularity over the last few years. (2) It features eggplant, zucchini, tomato, peppers, and garlic, chopped, mixed together, and cooked slowly over low heat. (3) Zucchini is a summer squash and has a smooth, dark green skin. (4) As the vegetables cook slowly, they make their own broth, which may be extended with a little tomato paste.

329. a. Sentence 1
b. Sentence 2
c. Sentence 3
d. Sentence 4

(1) An odd behavior associated with sleep and dreaming is somnambulism, commonly known as sleepwalking. (2) Sleepwalkers suffer from a malfunction in a brain mechanism that monitors the transition from REM to non-REM sleep. (3) REM sleep is vitally important to psychological well-being. (4) Sleepwalking episodes diminish with age and usually cause no serious harm—the worst thing that could happen would be a fall down the stairs.

330. a. Sentence 1
b. Sentence 2
c. Sentence 3
d. Sentence 4

(1) Lyme disease is sometimes called the "great imitator" because its many symptoms mimic those of other illnesses. (2) When treated, this disease usually presents few or no lingering effects. (3) Left untreated, it can be extremely debilitating and sometimes fatal. (4) One should be very careful when returning from a trek in the woods to check for deer ticks.

331. a. Sentence 1
b. Sentence 2
c. Sentence 3
d. Sentence 4

(1) During the next ten months, all bus operators with two or more years of service will be required to have completed twenty hours of refresher training on one of the Vehicle Maneuvering Training Buses (VMTB). (2) Instructors who have used this new technology report that trainees develop skills more quickly than with traditional training methods. (3) In refresher training, this new system reinforces defensive driving skills and safe driving habits. (4) The new VMTB are almost as much fun as a video game!

332. a. Sentence 1
b. Sentence 2
c. Sentence 3
d. Sentence 4

(1) In the summer, the northern hemisphere is slanted toward the sun, making the days longer and warmer than in winter. (2) Many religions make use of the solstices in their rites. (3) The first day of summer is called summer solstice and is also the longest day of the year. (4) However, June twenty-first marks the beginning of winter in the southern hemisphere, when that hemisphere is tilted away from the sun.

333.
  a. Sentence 1
  b. Sentence 2
  c. Sentence 3
  d. Sentence 4

(1) In TV detective shows the Internal Affairs Division officers are sometimes pictured as "the bad guys." (2) In many police departments, detectives who want to be promoted further must first spend an extended period of time working in the Internal Affairs division. (3) Not only do these officers become thoroughly versed in detecting police misconduct, they also become familiar with the circumstances and attitudes out of which such conduct might arise. (4) Placement in Internal Affairs reduces the possibility that a commanding officer might be too lenient in investigating or disciplining a colleague.

334.
  a. Sentence 1
  b. Sentence 2
  c. Sentence 3
  d. Sentence 4

(1) The park was empty, except for a child who stood just on the other side of the fence, a little girl about seven years old, thin and pale, with dark eyes and dark hair—cut short and ragged. (2) The statistics on neglected children in our country probably fall short of the actual numbers. (3) The child wore no coat, only a brown, cotton skirt that was too big for her—pinned at the waist with a safety pin—and a soiled, long-sleeved yellow blouse with rhinestone buttons. (4) Her fingernails were dirty and broken, the tips of her fingers bluish with cold.

335.
  a. Sentence 1
  b. Sentence 2
  c. Sentence 3
  d. Sentence 4

(1) Ghosts can be either benevolent or malevolent. (2) As someone once said, "I don't believe in ghosts, but I'm afraid of them." (3) They can be comic and comfortable, like the old sea captain in *The Ghost and Mrs. Muir*, or horrific beyond belief, like the ghosts of the revelers at the party in the Overlook Hotel in Stephen King's *The Shining*. (4) They can emerge from the afterlife to teach us lessons, like old Marley in *A Christmas Carol*, or come back moaning to be avenged, like the ghost in *Hamlet*.

336.
  a. Sentence 1
  b. Sentence 2
  c. Sentence 3
  d. Sentence 4

(1) Most criminals do not suffer from antisocial personality disorder; however, nearly all persons with this disorder have been in trouble with the law. (2) Sometimes labeled "sociopaths," they are a grim problem for society. (3) Their crimes range from con games to murder, and they are set apart by what appears to be a complete lack of conscience. (4) There is a long-standing debate among psychiatrists whether hardened criminals can ever truly be rehabilitated.

337. a. Sentence 1
b. Sentence 2
c. Sentence 3
d. Sentence 4

(1) Jessie Street is sometimes called the Australian Eleanor Roosevelt. (2) Eleanor Roosevelt was one of the most admired—and revered—women in history. (3) Like Roosevelt, Street lived a life of privilege, but at the same time devoted her efforts to working for the rights of the disenfranchised laborers, women, refugees, and Aborigines. (4) In addition, she gained international fame when she was the only woman on the Australian delegation to the conference that founded the United Nations—just as Eleanor Roosevelt was for the United States.

338. a. Sentence 1
b. Sentence 2
c. Sentence 3
d. Sentence 4

(1) Joining a health club allows you to exercise even when the weather is bad. (2) If you're a fitness walker, there is no need for a commute to a health club. (3) Your neighborhood can be your health club. (4) You don't need a lot of fancy equipment to get a good workout either. (5) All you need is a well-designed pair of athletic shoes.

339. a. Sentence 1
b. Sentence 2
c. Sentence 3
d. Sentence 4

(1) Members of your investigative team may have skills and abilities that you are not aware of. (2) As investigator in charge of a case, you should seek out and take advantage of potential talent in all the members of your team. (3) Positive reinforcement is an important motivator both for groups and for individuals. (4) Whenever a new case is given to your team, it is usually a good idea to have all the members come up with ideas and suggestions about all aspects of the case, rather than insisting that each member stick rigidly to his or her narrow area of expertise.

340. a. Sentence 1
b. Sentence 2
c. Sentence 3
d. Sentence 4

(1) Firefighters must learn the proper procedures for responding to residential carbon monoxide (CO) emergencies. (2) Upon arriving at the scene of the alarm, personnel shall put on protective clothing and then bring an operational, calibrated CO meter onto the premises. (3) CO poisoning can be lethal, both to firefighters and to ordinary citizens. (4) Occupants of the premises shall then be examined, and if they are experiencing CO poisoning symptoms—i.e., headaches, nausea, confusion, dizziness, and other flu-like symptoms—an Emergency Medical Services (EMS) crew shall be sent immediately to evacuate and administer oxygen to the occupants.

341. a. Sentence 1
b. Sentence 2
c. Sentence 3
d. Sentence 4

SET 31 (Answers begin on page 137.)
For each of the following groups of four numbered sentences, choose the sentence order that would result in the best paragraph.

(1) Figures have the power to mislead people. (2) Mathematics tells us about economic trends, patterns of disease, and the growth of populations. (3) Math is good at exposing the truth, but it can also perpetuate misunderstandings and untruths.

342. a. 1, 2, 3
b. 2, 3, 1
c. 3, 1, 2
d. 3, 2, 1

(1) The reason for so many injuries and fatalities is that a vehicle can generate heat of up to 1500°F. (2) Firefighters know that the dangers of motor-vehicle fires are too often overlooked. (3) In the United States, 1 out of 5 fires involves motor vehicles, resulting each year in 600 deaths, 2,600 civilian injuries, and 1,200 injuries to firefighters.

343. a. 1, 2, 3
b. 1, 3, 2
c. 2, 3, 1
d. 3, 2, 1

(1) Visits, especially from family members, can aid in a prisoner's rehabilitation. (2) Usually, this means that a prisoner and his visitors may not have physical contact with each other. (3) Therefore, they are separated by a pane of glass and must talk by phone. (4) However, in order to maintain prison safety, family visits cannot be unrestricted.

344. a. 2, 4, 1, 3
b. 1, 4, 2, 3
c. 1, 2, 3, 4
d. 3, 1, 2, 4

(1) But to keep the Peace Corps dynamic with fresh ideas, no staff member can work for the agency for more than five years. (2) People who work for the Peace Corps do so because they want to. (3) One of the missions of the Peace Corps is to help the people of interested countries meet their need for trained men and women.

345. a. 1, 2, 3
b. 3, 2, 1
c. 2, 3, 1
d. 3, 1, 2

(1) Leaving us behind in a bitter cloud of exhaust, the bus would cough and jolt down the narrow main street of Crossland. (2) Then, even before the bus got moving, she'd look away, ahead toward her real life. (3) But I could always imagine the way it would be once it got out on the open highway, gathered speed, and took Grandma back to a life as exotic to me as the deserts of Egypt. (4) When Grandma's visit was over, we'd take her down to the Greyhound station, watch her hand her ticket to the uniformed driver, disappear inside, and reappear to wave good-bye— her expression obscured by the bus's grimy window.

346. a. 4, 2, 1, 3
b. 4, 1, 3, 2
c. 1, 3, 4, 2
d. 1, 2, 3, 4

(1) The Fifth Amendment of the U.S. Constitution guarantees citizens freedom from double jeopardy in criminal proceedings. (2) It also means a person cannot be tried for a crime for which he has already been convicted; that is to say, a person convicted by a state court cannot be tried for the same offense in, for example, federal court. (3) Finally, a person cannot be punished more than once for the same crime. (4) This means that a person cannot be tried for a crime for which he has already been acquitted.

347. a. 1, 4, 2, 3
b. 1, 2, 4, 3
c. 3, 2, 1, 4
d. 3, 4, 2, 1

(1) If this is true, something must have happened to Mars billions of years ago that stripped away the planet's atmosphere. (2) These images also implied that Mars once had an atmosphere that was thick enough to trap the sun's heat. (3) Close-up images of Mars by the *Mariner 9* probe indicated networks of valleys that looked like the stream beds on Earth.

348. a. 2, 3, 1
b. 3, 1, 2
c. 3, 2, 1
d. 1, 3, 2

(1) Every spring the softball field became his favorite destination, and he had taken his son, Arnie, there when he was small to teach him how to pitch. (2) He walked home, as usual, through the park and, as usual, passed by the softball field. (3) This memory made him feel sad and guilty. (4) Arnie hadn't been in the least interested in softball, and so after two or three lessons he had given up the idea.

349. a. 2, 1, 4, 3
b. 3, 2, 1, 4
c. 4, 3, 1, 2
d. 2, 3, 4, 1

(1) If there are expenses incurred, complete report form 103; if there was damage to equipment, complete form 107. (2) If form 107 and form 103 are required, complete form 122 also. (3) Log on to the computer and go to the directory that contains the report forms. (4) As an employee, you must complete all paperwork.

350. a. 3, 2, 1, 4
b. 1, 3, 4, 2
c. 2, 1, 4, 3
d. 4, 3, 1, 2

(1) In some areas, the salt is combined with calcium chloride, which is more effective in below-zero temperatures and which melts ice better. (2) After a snow or icefall, city streets are treated with ordinary rock salt. (3) This combination of salt and calcium chloride is also less damaging to foliage along the roadways.

351. a. 2, 1, 3
b. 1, 3, 2
c. 3, 2, 1
d. 2, 3, 1

(1) Yet the human brain is the most mysterious and complex object on earth. (2) It has created poetry and music, planned and executed horrific wars, devised intricate scientific theories. (3) It thinks and dreams, plots and schemes, and easily holds more information than all the libraries on earth. (4) It weighs less than three pounds and is hardly more interesting to look at than an overly ripe cauliflower.

352. a. 1, 3, 4, 2
b. 2, 1, 4, 3
c. 3, 1, 2, 4
d. 4, 1, 2, 3

(1) Before you begin to compose a business letter, sit down and think about your purpose in writing the letter. (2) Do you want to request information, order a product, register a complaint, or apply for something? (3) Always keep your objective in mind. (4) Do some brainstorming and gather information before you begin writing.

353. a. 4, 3, 2, 1
b. 2, 4, 3, 1
c. 1, 2, 4, 3
d. 3, 2, 1, 4

(1) The idea communicated may even be purely whimsical, in which case the artist might start out with symbols developed from a bird's tracks or a child's toy. (2) Native American art often incorporates a language of abstract visual symbols. (3) The artist gives a poetic message to the viewer, communicating the beauty of an idea through religious symbols or by reproducing a design from nature—such as rain on leaves or sunshine on water.

354. a. 3, 1, 2
b. 2, 3, 1
c. 2, 1, 3
d. 1, 3, 2

(1) Japanese green tea is considered a gourmet treat by many tea drinkers, but it is much more than that. (2) Studies show that this relaxing drink may have disease-fighting properties. (3) Green tea inhibits some viruses and may protect people from heart disease.

355. a. 1, 2, 3
b. 2, 1, 3
c. 2, 3, 1
d. 3, 1, 2

SET 32 (Answers begin on page 138.)
Answer questions 356–358 on the basis of the following passage.

(1) Greyhound racing is the sixth most popular spectator sport in the United States. (2) Over the last decade, a growing number of racers have been adopted to live out retirement as household pets, once there racing career is over.

(3) Many people hesitate to adopt a retired racing greyhound because they think only very old dogs are available. (4) People also worry that the greyhound will be more nervous and active than other breeds and will need a large space to run. (5) _____. (6) In fact, racing greyhounds are put up for adoption at a young age; even champion racers, who have the longest careers, only work until they are about three-and-a-half years old. (7) Since greyhounds usually live to be 12–15 years old, their retirement is much longer than their racing careers. (8) Far from being nervous dogs, greyhounds have naturally

sweet, mild dispositions, and, while they love to run, they are sprinters rather than distance runners and are sufficiently exercised with a few laps around a fenced-in backyard everyday.

(9) Greyhounds do not make good watchdogs, but they are very good with children, get along well with other dogs (and usually cats as well), and are very affectionate and loyal. (10) A retired racing greyhound is a wonderful pet for almost anyone.

356. Which sentence, if inserted in the blank space labeled Part 5, would best help to focus the writer's argument in the second paragraph?
a. Even so, greyhounds are placid dogs.
b. These worries are based on false impressions and are easily dispelled.
c. Retired greyhounds do not need race tracks to keep in shape.
d. However, retired greyhounds are too old to need much exercise.

357. Which of the following changes is needed in the first paragraph?
a. Part 1: Change *growing* to *increasing*.
b. Part 2: Change *there* to *their*.
c. Part 1: Change *is* to *was*.
d. Part 2: Change *have been adopted* to *have adopted*.

358. Which of the following sentences, if added between Parts 9 and 10 of the third paragraph, would be most consistent with the writer's purpose, tone, and intended audience?
a. Former racing dogs make up approximately 0.36% of all dogs owned as domestic pets in the United States.
b. Despite the fact that greyhounds make excellent domestic pets, there is still a large number of former racers who have not been adopted.
c. Good-natured and tolerant dogs, greyhounds speedily settle into any household, large or small; they are equally at ease in an apartment or a private home.
d. It is imperative that people overcome the common myths they harbor about greyhounds that are preventing them from adopting these gentle dogs.

Answer questions 359–361 on the basis of the following paragraph.

    (1) Following a recent series of arson fires in public-housing buildings, the mayor of Crasonville has decided to expand the city's Community Patrol—made up of 18 to 21-year-olds—to about 400 people. (2) The Community Patrol has been an important part of the city's efforts to reduce the number of arson crimes.

    (3) In addition to the expanded patrol, the city also has decided to reduce the seriousness of these fires, most often set in stairwells, by stripping the paint from the stairwell walls. (4) Fed by the thick layers of oil-based paint, these arson fires race up the stairwells at an alarming speed.

    (5) Fire retardant failed to work in almost all cases. (6) When the city attempted to control the speed of these fires by covering walls with a flame retardant. (7) In the most recent fire, the flames raced up ten stories after the old paint under the newly applied fire retardant ignited. (8) Because the retardant failed to stop the flames, the city has decided to stop applying it and will now strip the stairwells down to the bare walls.

359. Which sentence in the third paragraph is a nonstandard sentence?
   a. Part 5
   b. Part 6
   c. Part 7
   d. Part 8

360. Which of the following changes should be made to Part 3 of the passage?
   a. Remove the word *also*.
   b. Change *patrol* to *patrols*.
   c. Change *has decided* to *decided*.
   d. Remove the word *these*.

361. Which of the following sentences, if inserted after Part 2 of the passage, would best develop the ideas in the first paragraph?
   a. The Community Patrol keeps up a twenty-four-hour-a-day watch of derelict buildings in four of the city's boroughs.
   b. The additional Community Patrol members effectively increase the Patrol's size by 25 percent.
   c. The Community Patrol has already reduced arson fires by 20 percent in certain neighborhoods; increasing the numbers of the Patrol will allow the city to extend this protection to all city boroughs.
   d. The increase in the Community Patrol also helps to lower unemployment among Crasonville's youth; this makes the increase a popular decision, enhancing the mayor's reputation with voters.

Answer questions 362 and 363 on the basis of the following passage.

(1) Yesterday I was exposed to what was called, in a recent newspaper ad for Dilly's Deli, "a dining experience like no other." (2) I decided on the hamburger steak special, the other specials were liver and onions and tuna casserole. (3) Each special is offered with two side dishes, but there was no potato salad left, and the green beans were cooked nearly beyond recognition. (4) I chose the gelatin of the day and what turned out to be the blandest coleslaw I have ever eaten.

(5) At Dilly's you sit at one of the four long tables. (6) The couple sitting across from me was having an argument. (7) The truck driver sitting next to me told me more than I wanted to know about highway taxes. (8) <u>After tasting</u> each of the dishes on my plate, it was time to leave; at that moment, one of the people working behind the counter yelled at me to clean up after myself. (9) Throwing away that plate of food was the most enjoyable part of dining at Dilly's.

362. Which of the following changes should be made to Part 2 of the first paragraph?
  a. Replace *were* with *are*.
  b. Replace the comma with a dash.
  c. Replace *I decided* with *Deciding*.
  d. Replace the comma with a semicolon.

363. Which of the following words or phrases should replace the underlined words in Part 8 of the second paragraph?
  a. Having tasted
  b. After I tasted
  c. Tasting
  d. After having tasted

SET 33 (Answers begin on page 139.)
Answer questions 364–366 on the basis of the following passage.

(1) Although most people are exercising regularly, experts note that eating right is also a key to good health. (2) Nutritionists recommend the "food pyramid" as a simple guide to eating the proper foods. (3) At the base of the food pyramid are grains and fiber. (4) People should eat six to eleven servings of bread, cereal, rice, and pasta everyday. (5) Servings of vegetables and fruit, the next level up the pyramid should be eaten five to nine times per day. (6) The next pyramid level is the dairy group. (7) Two or three servings a day of milk, yogurt, or cheese help maintain good nutrition. (8) Moving up the pyramid, the next level is the meat, poultry, fish, beans, eggs, and nuts group, of which everyone should eat only two to three servings a day. (9) At the very top of the pyramid is fats, oils, and sweets; these foods should be eaten only infrequently.

(10) _____. (11) If they follow the pyramid's guidelines, people do not have to shop in health food or specialty stores. (12) People need only stay in the outer 2 or 3 aisles of the supermarket, where the healthiest foods are located.

364. Which of the following revisions is necessary in Part 9 of the above passage?

a. At the very top of the pyramid is fats, oils and sweets; these foods should be eaten only infrequently.

b. At the very top of the pyramid are fats, oils, and sweets; these foods should be eaten only infrequently.

c. At the very top of the pyramid is fats, oils, and sweets; these foods must be eaten only infrequently.

d. At the very top of the pyramid is fats, oils, and sweets; only these foods should be eaten infrequently.

365. Which of the following sentences, if inserted in the blank line numbered Part 10, would be most consistent with the development and grammar of the paragraph?

a. The nutrition plan set out in the food pyramid was designed to make it easy to fit good nutrition habits into your already too complicated lives.

b. Unlike fad diets and weighty books of calorie counts, the food pyramid is a clear visual aid that will help people remember the essentials of healthy eating.

c. While the food pyramid can help you learn how to eat more healthily, it cannot replace the necessity of exercise.

d. The nutrition plan set out in the food pyramid was designed to make it easy to fit good nutrition habits into people's already too complicated lives.

366. Which of the following changes is needed in the above passage?

a. Part 5: Insert comma after *pyramid*.

b. Part 1: Replace *most* with *more*.

c. Part 7: Replace *of which* with *which*.

d. Part 8: Insert a colon after *is*.

Answer questions 367 and 368 on the basis of the following passage.

> (1) Police officers must read suspects their Miranda rights upon taking them into custody. (2) When a suspect who is merely being questioned <u>incriminates</u> himself, he might later claim to have been in custody and seek to have the case dismissed on the grounds of not having been <u>appraised</u> of his Miranda rights. (3) In such cases, a judge must make a determination as to whether or not a reasonable person would have believed himself to have been in custody, based on certain <u>criteria</u>. (4) Officers must be aware of these criteria and take care not to give suspects grounds for later claiming they believed themselves to be in custody. (5) The judge must <u>ascertain</u> whether the suspect was questioned in a threatening manner (threatening could mean that the suspect was seated while both officers remained standing) and whether the suspect was aware that he or she was free to leave at any time.

367. Which of the underlined words in the paragraph should be replaced by a more appropriate, accurate word?
   a. incriminates
   b. appraised
   c. criteria
   d. ascertain

368. Which of the following changes would make the sequence of ideas in the paragraph clearer?
   a. Place Part 5 after Part 1.
   b. Reverse Parts 3 and 5.
   c. Reverse the order of Parts 4 and 5.
   d. Delete Part 2.

Answer questions 369 and 370 on the basis of the following passage.

(1) In space flight there are the obvious hazards of meteors, debris, and radiation, however, astronauts must also deal with two vexing physiological foes—muscle atrophy and bone loss. (2) Space shuttle astronauts, because they spend only about a week in space, undergo minimal wasting of bone and muscle. (3) But when longer stays in microgravity or zero gravity are contemplated, as in the proposed space station or a two-year round trip voyage to Mars, these problems are of particular concern because they could become acute.

(4) One completed NASA study, as well as a preliminary experiment at MIT, show that muscle atrophy can be kept largely at bay with appropriate exercise, but bone loss caused by reduced gravity cannot. (5) The scientists can measure certain flight-related hormonal changes and can obtain animal bone biopsies immediately after flights, but they do not completely understand how gravity affects the bones or what happens at the cellular level.

369. Which of the following parts of the passage is a nonstandard sentence?
   a.   Part 1
   b.   Part 3
   c.   Part 4
   d.   Part 5

370. Which of the following changes is needed in the passage?
   a.   Part 3: Change *they* to *it*.
   b.   Part 4: Change *flight-related* to *flight related*.
   c.   Part 4: Change *show* to *shows*.
   d.   Part 5: Change *they do* to *he does*.

Answer questions 371 and 372 on the basis of the following passage.

(1) An ecosystem is a group of animals and plants living in a specific region and interacting with one another and with their physical environment. (2) Ecosystems include physical and chemical components, such as soils, water, and nutrients that support the organisms living there. (3) These organisms may range from large animals to microscopic bacteria. (4) Ecosystems also can be thought of as the interactions among all organisms in a given habitat; for instance, one species may serve as food for another. (5) People are part of the ecosystems where they live and work. (6) Environmental Groups are forming in many communities. (7) Human activities can harm or destroy local ecosystems unless actions such as land development for housing or businesses are carefully planned to conserve and sustain the ecology of the area. (8) An important part of ecosystem management involves finding ways to protect and enhance economic and social well-being while protecting local ecosystems.

371. Which of the following numbered parts is LEAST relevant to the main idea of the paragraph?

a. Part 1
b. Part 6
c. Part 7
d. Part 8

372. Which of the following changes is needed in the passage?

a. Part 5: Place a comma after *live*.
b. Part 2: Remove the comma after *water*.
c. Part 6: Use a lower case *g* for the word *Group*.
d. Part 8: Change *involves* to *involved*.

Answer questions 373–374 on the basis of the following passage.

(1) There are two types of diabetes, insulin-dependent and non-insulin-dependent. (2) Between 90 and 95 percent of the estimated 13 to 14 million people in the United States with diabetes have non-insulin-dependent, or Type II, diabetes. (3) Because this form of diabetes usually begins in adults over the age of 40 and is most common after the age of 55, it used to be called adult-onset diabetes. (4) _____ its symptoms often develop gradually and are hard to identify at first, nearly half of all people with diabetes do not know they have it. (5) _____, someone who has developed Type II diabetes may more feel tired or ill without knowing why. (6) This can be particularly dangerous because untreated diabetes can cause damage to the heart, blood vessels, eyes, kidneys, and

nerves. (7) While the causes, short-term effects, and treatments of the two types of diabetes differ, both types can cause the same long-term health problems.

373. Which of the following parts of the paragraph contains a nonstandard comparison?

a. Part 7
b. Part 5
c. Part 3
d. Part 2

374. Which sequence of words, if inserted in order into the blanks in the paragraph, help the reader understand the sequence and logic of the writer's ideas?

a. Since . . . For example
b. While . . . Next
c. Moreover . . . Eventually
d. Because . . . Thus

SET 34 (Answers begin on page 141.)
Answer questions 375–377 on the basis of the following paragraph.

(1) By using tiny probes as neural prostheses, scientists may be able to restore nerve function in quadriplegics, make the blind see, or the deaf hear. (2) Thanks to advanced techniques, an implanted probe can stimulate individual neurons electrically or chemically and then record responses. (3) Preliminary results suggest that the microprobe telemetry systems can be permanently implanted and replace damaged or missing nerves.

(4) The tissue-compatible microprobes represent an advance over the typically aluminum wire electrodes used in studies of the cortex and other brain structures. (5) Previously, researchers data were accumulated using traditional electrodes, but there is a question of how much damage they cause to the nervous system. (6) Microprobes, since they are slightly thinner than a human hair, cause minimal damage and disruption of neurons when inserted into the brain because of their diminutive width.

(7) In addition to recording nervous system impulses, the microprobes have minuscule channels that open the way for delivery of drugs, cellular growth factors, neurotransmitters, and other neuroactive compounds to a single neuron or to groups of neurons. (8) The probes usually have up to four channels, each with its own recording/stimulating electrode.

375. Which of the following changes is needed in the above passage?
- a. Part 8: Change *its* to *it's*.
- b. Part 6: Change *their* to *its*.
- c. Part 6: Change *than* to *then*.
- d. Part 5: Change *researchers* to *researchers'*.

376. Which of the following includes a nonstandard use of an adverb in the passage?
- a. Part 2
- b. Part 4
- c. Part 6
- d. Part 8

377. Which of the following numbered parts should be revised to reduce unnecessary repetition?
- a. Part 2
- b. Part 5
- c. Part 6
- d. Part 8

Answer questions 378–380 on the basis of the following passage.

(1) Loud noises on trains not only irritate passengers but also create unsafe situations. (2) They are prohibited by law and by agency policy. (3) Therefore, conductors follow the procedures outlined below:

(4) A passenger-created disturbance is by playing excessively loud music or creating loud noises in some other manner. (5) In the event a passenger creates a disturbance, the conductor will politely ask the passenger to turn off the music or stop making the loud noise. (6) If the passenger refuses to comply, the conductor will tell the passenger that he or she is in violation of the law and train policy and will have to leave the train if he or she will not comply to the request. (7) If police assistance is requested, the conductor will stay at the location from which the call to the Command Center was placed or the silent alarm used. (8) Conductors will wait there until the police arrive, will allow passengers to get off the train at this point, and no passengers are allowed back on until the situation is resolved.

378. Which of the following numbered parts contains a nonstandard sentence?
a. Part 3
b. Part 4
c. Part 6
d. Part 7

379. Which of the following sentences is the best revision of the sentence numbered Part 8 in the passage?
a. Conductors will wait there until the police arrive, will allow passengers off the train at this point, and no passengers will be allowed on until the situation is resolved.
b. Conductors will wait there until the police arrive, will allow passengers off the train at this point, and, until the situation is resolved, no passengers are allowed on.
c. Conductors will wait there until the police arrive, will allow passengers off the train at this point, and will not allow passengers on until the situation is resolved.
d. Conductors will wait there until the police arrive, will allow passengers off the train at this point, and no passengers will be allowed on until the situation is resolved.

380. Which of the following numbered parts contains a nonstandard use of a preposition?
a. Part 2
b. Part 6
c. Part 7
d. Part 8

Answer questions 381–383 on the basis of the following passage.

(1) In his State of the Union address (February 4, 1997), President Clinton challenged America to make the 13th and 14th years of education—at least two years of college—as universal in this country as high school is today. (2) His plan includes five tax benefits for middle-class students and families that pursue additional education for their children and they. (3) The proposed HOPE Scholarship tax credit which offers two years of tuition at the typical community college for any student enrolled at least half-time. (4) The government will institute a tax deduction of up to $10,000 per family per year for tuition and fees (minus grants) for college, graduate school, community college, and certified training and technical programs. (5) Families will have the flexibility to use funds in Individual Retirement Accounts for post-secondary education expenses free from early withdrawal tax penalties. (6) There will be a change in the tax law, so more students will be able to use community or public service to repay their student loans without owing tax. (7) Finally, the government will be reinstating, through the year 2000, the current exclusion from an employee's income of up to $5,250 per year of postsecondary educational assistance provided by an employer for undergraduate and graduate students.

381. Which of the following numbered parts contains a nonstandard sentence?
   a.   Part 3
   b.   Part 6
   c.   Part 2
   d.   Part 5

382. Which of the following sentences, if inserted between Part 2 and Part 3 of the passage, would best focus the purpose of the writer?
   a.   While the proposals would be helpful for middle class families, they are unlikely to be of benefit to low-income households.
   b.   Extending the length of universal education in this country will make the United States a stronger force than ever in competitive world markets.
   c.   The following is a brief description of each of the five proposals.
   d.   Lowering taxes on middle-income families is the only viable method of increasing the duration of universal education in the United States of America.

383. Which of the following changes needs to be made to the above passage?
   a.   Part 1: Change *as universal* to *more universal*.
   b.   Part 2: Change *they* to *themselves*.
   c.   Part 6: Change *to repay* to *repay*.
   d.   Part 7: Change *reinstating* to *instituting*.

Answer questions 384–387 on the basis of the following passage.

(1) A report on 1996 dropout rates in the United States released by the U.S. Department of Education's National Center for Education Statistics found that more young adults are completing high school through alternative methods; such as the GED.

(2)"Alternative programs that give young people a second chance are a growing phenomena," says U.S. Secretary of Education Richard W. Riley. (3) "We need to develop more, higher quality alternative programs than meet this rising demand. (4) Young people at risk should not just be left on their own to hang out on the street. (5) New attention needs to be paid to finding ways to encourage many more dropouts to drop back in to school so that they have a real chance at living a decent life. (6) When young people drop out, they do more than just give up their education, they are, too often, giving up on themselves."

384. Which of the following changes needs to be made to the above passage?

a. Part 3: remove the comma after *more*.

b. Part 1: insert a comma after *statistics*.

c. Part 4: change *their* to *there*.

d. Part 3: change *than* to *that*.

385. Which of the following numbered parts contains a nonstandard sentence?

a. Part 5

b. Part 6

c. Part 1

d. Part 2

386. Which of the following numbered parts contains a nonstandard sentence?

a. Part 1

b. Part 4

c. Part 6

d. Part 2

387. Which of the following should be used in place of the underlined word in Part 2 of the first paragraph?

a. Educational

b. Education's

c. Educations'

d. Educated

SET 35 (Answers begin on page 142.)
Answer questions 388–390 on the basis of the following passage.

(1) <u>Rigorous</u> math courses, like algebra and geometry, are a <u>gateway</u> to college and to future employment, U.S. Secretary of Education Richard W. Riley said recently.

(2) Riley said the Third International Mathematics and Science Study (TIMSS) found U.S. students above the international <u>average</u> in both math and science in the 4th grade, but slipping <u>a lot</u> in math by the 8th grade.

(3) "We need to end this slide, and we can start to do it by putting the spotlight on what is happening in middle school math classes, Riley said. (4) "So one of my messages to schools and parents is very simple: push all of your students to take the gateway courses and give them the opportunity to use all of their God-given abilities. (5) Do not give up on any child. (6) Start giving young people the opportunity to take algebra in the eighth grade. (7) Students who start this subject early go on to take chemistry, calculus, physics, and the other courses that give them the solid grounding for success in college and careers."

388. Which of the following changes is needed in the third paragraph?
   a. Part 4: Remove the quotation marks before *So*.
   b. Part 7: Insert a comma after *early*.
   c. Part 3: Insert quotation marks after *classes*.
   d. Part 5: Change *on* to *to*.

389. Which of the underlined words or phrases in the passage should be replaced by more precise or appropriate words?
   a. gateway
   b. rigorous
   c. average
   d. a lot

390. Which of the following editorial changes would help focus attention on the main idea on the third paragraph?
   a. Reverse the order of Part 5 and Part 7.
   b. Delete Part 6.
   c. Combine Part 5 and 6 into one sentence.
   d. Make the second paragraph the first sentence of the third paragraph.

Answer questions 391–393 on the basis of the following passage.

(1) If you have little time to care for your garden, be sure to select hardy plants, such as phlox, comfrey, and peonies. (2) These will, with only a little care, keep the garden brilliant with color all through the growing season. (3) Sturdy sunflowers and hardy species of roses are also good selections. (4) As a thrifty gardener, you should leave part of the garden free for the planting of herbs such as lavender, sage, thyme, and parsley.

(5) If you have a moderate amount of time, growing vegetables and a garden culture of pears, apples, quinces, and other small fruits can be an interesting occupation, which amply rewards the care languished on it. (6) Even a small vegetable and fruit garden may yield radishes, celery, beans, and strawberries that will be delicious on the family table. (7) _____. (8) When planting seeds for the vegetable garden, you should be sure that they receive the proper amount of moisture, that they are sown at the right season to receive the right degree of heat, and that the seed is placed near enough to the surface to allow the young plant to reach the light easily.

391. Which of the following editorial changes would best help to clarify the ideas in the first paragraph?
   a. Omit the phrase, *with only a little care*, from Part 2.
   b. Reverse the order of Parts 2 and 3.
   c. Add a sentence after Part 4 explaining why saving room for herbs is a sign of thrift in a gardener.
   d. Add a sentence about the ease of growing roses after Part 3.

392. Which of the following sentences, if inserted in the blank line numbered Part 7, would be most consistent with the writer's development of ideas in the second paragraph?
   a. When and how you plant is important to producing a good yield from your garden.
   b. Very few gardening tasks are more fascinating than growing fruit trees.
   c. Of course, if you have saved room for an herb garden, you will be able to make the yield of your garden even more tasty by cooking with your own herbs.
   d. Growing a productive fruit garden may take some specialized and time-consuming research into proper grafting techniques.

393. Which of the following changes needs to be made in the above passage?
   a. Part 2: Change *through* to *threw*.
   b. Part 5: Change *languished* to *lavished*.
   c. Part 8: Change *sown* to *sewn*.
   d. Part 8: Change *surface* to *surfeit*.

Answer questions 394 and 395 on the basis of the following passage.

This selection is from Willa Cather's short story, "Neighbor Rosicky."

(1) On the day before Christmas the weather set in very cold; no snow, but a bitter, biting wind that whistled and sang over the flat land and lashed one's face like fine wires. (2) There was baking going on in the Rosicky kitchen all day, and Rosicky sat inside, making over a coat that Albert had outgrown into an overcoat for John. (3) Mary's big red geranium in bloom for Christmas, and a row of Jerusalem cherry trees, full of berries. (4) It was the first year she had ever grown these; Doctor Ed brung her the seeds from Omaha when he went to some medical convention. (5) They reminded Rosicky of plants he had seen in England; and all afternoon, as he stitched, he sat thinking about the two years in London, which his mind usually shrank from even after all this while.

394. Which of the following numbered parts displays nonstandard use of a verb form?
   a. Part 2
   b. Part 3
   c. Part 4
   d. Part 5

395. Which of the following numbered parts contains a nonstandard sentence?
   a. Part 2
   b. Part 3
   c. Part 4
   d. Part 5

SET 36 (Answers begin on page 143.)
Answer questions 396–398 on the basis of the following passage.

(1) Augustus Saint-Gaudens was born March 1, 1848, in Dublin, Ireland, to Bernard Saint-Gaudens, a French shoemaker, and Mary McGuinness, his Irish wife. (2) Six months later, the family immigrated to New York City, where Augustus grew up. (3) Upon completion of school at age thirteen, he expressed strong interest in art as a career so his father apprenticed him to a cameo cutter. (4) While working days at his cameo lathe, Augustus also took art classes at the Cooper Union and the National Academy of Design.

(5) At 19, his apprenticeship completed, Augustus traveled to Paris where he studied under Francois Jouffry at the renown Ecole des Beaux-Arts. (6) In 1870, he left Paris for Rome, where for the next five years, he <u>studies</u> classical art and architecture, and worked on his first commissions. (7) In 1876, he received his first major commission—a monument to Civil War Admiral David Glasgow Farragut. (8) Unveiled in New York's Madison Square in 1881, the monument was a tremendous success; its combination of realism and allegory was a departure from previous American sculpture. (9) Saint-Gaudens' fame grew, and other commissions were quickly forthcoming.

396. Which of the following numbered parts requires a comma to separate two independent clauses?

a. Part 1
b. Part 3
c. Part 7
d. Part 9

397. Which of the following words should replace the underlined word in Part 6?

a. studied
b. will study
c. had been studying
d. would have studied

398. Which of the following changes needs to be made to the passage?

a. Part 2: Change *where* to *when*.
b. Part 5: Change *renown* to *renowned*.
c. Part 8: Change *its* to *it's*.
d. Part 3: Change *expressed* to *impressed*.

Answer questions 399–401 on the basis of the following passage.

(1) Everglades National Park is the largest remaining sub-tropical wilderness in the continental United States. (2) It is home to abundant wildlife; including alligators, crocodiles, manatees, and Florida panthers. (3) The climate of the Everglades are mild and pleasant from December through April, though rare cold fronts may create near freezing conditions. (4) Summers are hot and humid; in summer, the temperatures often soar to around 90 degrees and the humidity climbs to over 90 percent. (5) Afternoon thunderstorms are common, and mosquitoes are abundant.

(6) If you visit the Everglades, wear comfortable sportswear in winter; loose-fitting, long-sleeved shirts and pants, and insect repellent are recommended in the summer.

(7) Walking and canoe trails, boat tours, and tram tours are excellent for viewing wildlife, including alligators and a multitude of tropical and temperate birds. (8) Camping, whether in the back country or at established campgrounds, offers the opportunity to enjoy what the park offers firsthand. (9) Year-round, ranger-led activities may help you to enjoy your visit even more; such activities are offered throughout the park in all seasons.

399. Which of the following numbered parts contains a nonstandard use of a semicolon?

a. Part 6
b. Part 2
c. Part 9
d. Part 4

400. Which of the following numbered parts needs to be revised to reduce unnecessary repetition?

a. Part 4
b. Part 6
c. Part 9
d. Part 8

401. Which of the following changes is needed in the above passage?

a. Part 2: Change *it's* to *its*.
b. Part 3: Change *are* to *is*.
c. Part 6: Remove the comma after *Everglades*.
d. Part 8: Remove the comma after *campgrounds*.

Answer questions 402 and 403 on the basis of the following passage.

(1) The Food and Drug Administration (FDA) today announced that starting January 1, 1998, lower-fat milk products must follow the same set of criteria as most other foods labeled "low fat." (2) This means that such products as 2-percent milk, which contain about 5 grams of fat per serving, cannot be labeled "low fat" because the fat content is more than 3 grams per serving, the upper limit permitted in food products labeled "low fat." (3) The Surgeon General advises that low-fat and high-fiber diets will help to improve the health of Americans and reduce medical costs to the country. (4) The FDA judged that the designation "2% fat" on reduced fat milk products was causing consumers to imply that such products were actually low in fat content.

(5) As the new year begins, the new ruling will help improve the health of all Americans. (6) Milk is crucial to good nutrition, and now consumers can fit it into low-fat diets.

402. Which of the following numbered parts is least relevant to the first paragraph?
  a. Part 1
  b. Part 2
  c. Part 3
  d. Part 4

403. Which of the following changes needs to be made to the above passage?
  a. Part 4: Change *imply* to *infer*.
  b. Part 6: Change *crucial* to *crucially*.
  c. Part 1: Change *criteria* to *criterion*.
  d. Part 4: Change *designation* to *assignation*.

Answer questions 404–406 on the basis of the following passage.

(1) Being able to type good is no longer a requirement limited to secretaries and novelists; thanks to the computer, anyone who wants to enter the working world needs to be <u>accustomed</u> to a keyboard. (2) Just knowing your way around a keyboard does not mean that you can use one efficiently, though; while you may have progressed beyond the "hunt-and-peck" method, you may never have learned to type quickly and accurately. (3) Doing so is a skill that will not only ensure that you pass a typing <u>proficiency</u> exam, but one that is essential if you want to advance your career in any number of fields. (4) This chapter <u>assures</u> that you are familiar enough with a standard keyboard to be able to use it without looking at the keys, which is the first step in learning to type, and that you are aware of the proper <u>fingering</u>. (5) The following information will help you to increase your speed and accuracy and to do our best when being tested on timed writing passages.

404. Which of the following numbered parts contains a nonstandard use of a modifier?

a. Part 1

b. Part 2

c. Part 3

d. Part 5

405. Which of the following words, underlined in the above passage, is misused in its context?

a. assures

b. proficiency

c. fingering

d. accustomed

406. Which of the following changes needs to be made in the passage?

a. Part 3: Remove the comma after *exam*.

b. Part 4: Insert a colon after *that*.

c. Part 1: Change *needs* to *needed*.

d. Part 5: Change *our* to *your*.

SET 37 (Answers begin on page 144.)

Answer questions 407 and 408 on the basis of the following passage.

(1) None of us knew my Uncle Elmer, not even my mother (he would have been ten years older than she) we had pictures of him in an ancient family album, a solemn, spindly baby, dressed in a white muslin shirt, ready for bed, or in a sailor suit, holding a little drum. (2) In one photo-graph, he stands in front of a tall chiffonier, which looms behind him, massive and shadowy, like one of the Fates in a greek play. (3) There weren't many such pictures, because photographs weren't easy to come by in those days, and in the ones we did have, my uncle had a formal posed look, as if, even then, he knew he was bound for some unique destiny. (4) It was the summer I turned thirteen that I found out what happened to him, the summer Sister Mattie Fisher, one of Grandma's evangelist friends, paid us a visit, sweeping in like a cleansing wind and telling the truth.

407. Which of the following changes needs to be made to the above passage?

a. Part 2: Change *greek* to *Greek*.

b. Part 4: Change *Sister* to *sister*.

c. Part 4: Change *summer* to *Summer*.

d. Part 3: Change *uncle* to *Uncle*.

408. Which of the following numbered parts contains a nonstandard sentence?

a. Part 1

b. Part 2

c. Part 3

d. Part 4

Answer questions 409–411 on the basis of the following passage.

(1) O'Connell Street is the main thoroughfare of Dublin City. (2) Although it is not a particularly long street Dubliners will tell the visitor proudly that it is the widest street in all of Europe. (3) This claim usually meets with protests, especially from French tourists who claim The Champs Elysees of Paris as Europe's widest street. (4) But the witty Dubliner will not <u>ensign</u> bragging rights easily and will trump the French visitor with a fine distinction: the Champs Elysees is the widest boulevard, but O'Connell is the widest street.

(5) Divided by several important monuments running the length of its center, the street is named for Daniel O'Connell, an Irish patriot. (6) An impressive monument to him towers over the entrance of lower O'Connell Street and overlooking the Liffey River. (7) O'Connell stands high above the unhurried crowds of shoppers, business people, and students on a sturdy column; he is surrounded by four serene angels seated at each corner of the monument's base.

409. Which of the following words should replace the underlined word in Part 4 of the passage?
a. require
b. relinquish
c. acquire
d. assign

410. Which of the following changes needs to be made to the second paragraph of the passage?

a. Part 7: Replace the semicolon with a comma.
b. Part 5: Change *Irish* to *irish*.
c. Part 5: Change *running* to *run*.
d. Part 6: Change *overlooking* to *overlooks*.

411. Which of the following changes needs to be made to the first paragraph of the passage?
a. Part 2: Insert a comma after *that*.
b. Part 3: Replace the comma after *protests* with a semicolon.
c. Part 4: Remove the colon after *distinction*.
d. Part 2: Insert a comma after *street*.

Answer questions 412–414 on the basis of the following passage.

(1) Mrs. Lake arriving twenty minutes early surprised and irritated Nicholas, although the moment for saying so slipped past too quickly for him to snatch its opportunity.

(2) She was a thin woman of medium height, not much older than he—in her middle forties he judged—dressed in a red-and-white, polka-dot dress and open-toed red shoes with extremely high heels. (3) Her short brown hair was crimped in waves, which gave a incongruous, quaint, old-fashioned effect. (4) She had a pointed nose. (5) Her eyes, set rather shallow, were light brown and inquisitive.

(6) "Dr. Markley?" she asked. (7) Nicholas nodded, and the woman walked in past him, proceeding with little mincing steps to the center of the living room where she stood with her back turned, looking around. (8) "My my," she said. (9) "This is

a nice house. (**10**) Do you live here all alone?"

412. Which of the following changes should be made in Part 3?
   a. Change *was* to *is*.
   b. Change *gave* to *gives*.
   c. Change *a* to *an*.
   d. Change *effect* to *affect*.

413. Which of the following numbered parts contains a nonstandard use of a modifier?
   a. Part 7
   b. Part 5
   c. Part 3
   d. Part 2

414. Which of the following changes needs to be made to Part 1?
   a. Insert a comma after *early*.
   b. Change *too* to *two*.
   c. Change *Lake* to *Lake's*.
   a. Change *its* to *it's*.

SET 38 (Answers begin on page 145.)
Answer questions 415–417 on the basis of the following passage.

(1) If your office job involves telephone work, than your voice may be the first contact a caller has to your company or organization. (2) For this reason, your telephone manners have to be impeccable. (3) Always answer the phone promptly, on the first or second ring, if possible. (4) Speak directly into the phone, neither too loudly nor too softly, in a pleasant, cheerful voice. (5) Vary the pitch of your voice, so that it will not sound monotonous or uninterested, and be sure to enunciate clearly. (6) After a short, friendly greeting,

state your company or boss's name, then your own name.

(7) Always take messages carefully. (8) Fill out all pertinent blanks on the message pad sheet while you are still on the phone. (9) Always let the caller hang up first. (10) Do not depend in your memory for the spelling of a name or the last digit of a phone number, and be sure to write legibly. (11) When it is time to close a conversation, do so in a pleasant manner, and never hang up without saying good-bye. (12) While it is not an absolute rule, generally closing with *Good bye* is more professional than *bye-bye*. (13) Verify the information by reading it back to the caller.

415. Which of the following editorial changes would most improve the clarity of development of ideas in the second paragraph?
   a. Delete Part 9.
   b. Reverse the order of Part 8 and Part 13.
   c. Reverse the order of Part 9 and Part 13.
   d. Add a sentence after Part 7 explaining the need to take phone messages from customers politely.

416. Which of the following changes needs to be made to the first paragraph?
   a. Part 5: Change *they* to *it*.
   b. Part 1: Change *than* to *then*.
   c. Part 2: Change *manners* to *manner*.
   d. Part 6: Change *boss's* to *bosses*.

417. Which of the following numbered parts contains a nonstandard use of a preposition?
   a. Part 1
   b. Part 2
   c. Part 8
   d. Part 10

Answer questions 418 and 419 on the basis of the following passage.

(1) Understand that your boss has problems, too. (2) This is easy to forget. (3) When someone has authority over you, it's hard to remember that they're just human. (4) Your boss may have children at home who misbehave, dogs or cats or parakeets that need to go to the vet, deadlines to meet, and/or bosses of his or her own (sometimes even bad ones) overseeing his or her work. (5) If your boss is occasionally unreasonable, try to keep in mind that it might have nothing to do with you. (6) He or she may be having a bad day for reasons no one else knows. (7) Of course if such behavior becomes consistently abusive, you'll have to do something about it—confront the problem or even quit. (8) But were all entitled to occasional mood swings.

418. Which of the following numbered parts contains a nonstandard use of a pronoun?
   a. Part 3
   b. Part 4
   c. Part 7
   d. Part 8

419. Which of the following changes needs to be made to the above passage?
   a. Part 5: Change *unreasonable* to *unreasonably*.
   b. Part 7: Change the dash to a semicolon.
   c. Part 8: Change *were* to *we're*.
   d. Part 4: Change *deadlines* to *a deadline*.

Answer questions 420 and 421 on the basis of the following passage.

(1) Kwanzaa is a holiday celebrated by many African-Americans from December 26th through January 1st. (2) It pays tribute to the rich cultural roots of Americans of African ancestry, and celebrates family, community, and culture, Kwanzaa means *the first* or *the first fruits of the harvest* and is based on the ancient African first-fruit harvest celebrations. (3) The modern holiday of Kwanzaa was founded in 1966 by Dr. Maulana Karenga, a professor at California State University in Long Beach, California. (4) The seven-day celebration encourages people to think about their African roots as well as their life in present day America.

420. Which of the following sentences would be the best topic sentence for a second paragraph on the same subject?
   a. The seven fundamental principles on which Kwanzaa is based are referred to as the *Nguzo Saba*.
   b. These rules consist of unity, self-determination, collective work and responsibility, cooperative economics, purpose, creativity, and faith.
   c. Each of its seven candles represents a distinct principle beginning with unity, the center candle.
   d. Participants celebrate by performing rituals such as lighting the kinara.

421. Which of the following numbered parts in the passage contains a nonstandard sentence?
a. Part 4
b. Part 3
c. Part 1
d. Part 2

Answer questions 422 and 423 on the basis of the following passage.

(1) Beginning next month, City Transit will institute the Stop Here Program, who will be in effect every night from 10:00 P.M. until 4:00 A.M. (2) The program will allow drivers to stop the bus wherever a passenger wishes, as long as they deem it is safe to stop there. (3) This program will reduce the amount of walking that passengers will have to do after dark. (4) Passengers may request a stop anywhere along the bus route by pulling the bell cord a block ahead. (5) During the first two months of the program, when passengers attempt to flag down a bus anywhere but at a designated stop, the bus driver should proceed to the next stop and wait for them to board the bus. (6) Then the driver should give the passenger a brochure that explains the Stop Here Program.

422. Which of the following editorial changes in the above passage would best help to clarify the information the paragraph intends to convey?
a. Add a sentence between Parts 4 and 5 explaining that while the Stop Here Program allows passengers to leave the bus at almost any point, passengers may board only at designated stops.
b. Delete Part 6.
c. Add a sentence between Parts 5 and 6 explaining the safety advantages for passengers of flagging down buses at night.
d. Reverse the order of Parts 4 and 5.

423. Which of the following numbered parts contains a nonstandard use of a pronoun?
a. Part 1
b. Part 2
c. Part 3
d. Part 5

Answer questions 424 and 425 on the basis of the following passage.

(1) In October of 1993, a disastrous wildfire swept across portions of Charlesburg. (2) Five residents were killed, 320 homes destroyed, and 19,500 acres burned. (3) A public safety task force was formed to review emergency choice. (4) The task force findings were as follows.

(5) The water supply in the residential areas was insufficient, some hydrants could not even be opened. (6) The task force recommended a review of hydrant inspection policy.

(7) The fire companies that responded had difficulty locating specific sites. (8) Most companies came from other areas and were not familiar with Charlesburg. (9) The available maps were outdated and did not reflect recent housing developments.

(10) Evacuation procedures were inadequate. (11) Residents reported being given conflicting and/or confusing information. (12) Some residents of the Hilltop Estates subdivision ignored mandatory evacuation orders, yet others were praised for their cooperation.

424. Which of the following numbered parts contains a nonstandard sentence?
a. Part 7
b. Part 5
c. Part 3
d. Part 12

425. Which of the following changes needs to be made to the passage?
a. Part 12: Change *their* to *they're*.
b. Part 12: Insert a comma after *others*.
c. Part 2: Remove the comma after *killed*.
d. Part 4: Replace the semicolon with a colon.

SET 39 (Answers begin on page 146.)
Answer questions 426–428 on the basis of the following passage.

(1) In 1519, Hernando cortez led his army of Spanish Conquistadors into Mexico. (2) Equipped with horses, shining armor, and the most advanced weapons of the sixteenth century, he fought his way from the flat coastal area into the mountainous highlands. (3) Cortez was looking for gold, and he were sure that Indian groups in Mexico had mined large amounts of the precious metal. (4) First, he conquered the groups and then seized their precious gold using very organized methods.

426. Which of the underlined words in the passage above could be replaced with a more precise verb?
a. was looking
b. equipped
c. conquered
d. seized

427. Which of the following sentences uses the verb incorrectly?
- a. Part 1
- b. Part 2
- c. Part 3
- d. Part 4

428. Which of the following changes needs to be made to the above passage?
- a. Part 2: Delete the comma after *horses*.
- b. Part 1: Capitalize the *c* in *Cortez*.
- c. Part 3: Insert a comma after *groups*.
- d. Part 4: Place a semicolon after *groups*.

Answer questions 429 and 430 on the basis of the following passage.

(1) Charles Darwin was born in 1809 at Shrewsbury England. (2) He was a biologist whose famous theory of evolution is important to philosophy for the effects it has had about the nature of man. (3) After many years of careful study, Darwin attempted to show that higher species had come into existence as a result of the gradual transformation of lower species; and that the process of transformation could be explained through the selective effect of the natural environment upon organisms.

(4) He concluded that the principles of *natural selection* and *survival of the fittest* govern all life. (5) Darwin's explanation of these principles is that because of the food supply problem, the young born to any species compete for survival. (6) Those young that survive to produce the next generation tend to embody favorable natural changes which are then passed on by heredity. (7) His major work that contained these theories is *On the Origin of the Species* written in 1859. Many religious opponents condemned this work.

429. Which of the following corrections should be made in punctuation?
- a. Part 4: Insert a comma before *and*.
- b. Part 3: Delete the comma after *study*.
- c. Part 2: Insert quotation marks around *nature of man*.
- d. Part 1: Insert a comma after *Shrewsbury*.

430. In Part 7 *On the Origin of Species* is italicized because it is
- a. a short story.
- b. the title of a book.
- c. name of the author.
- d. copyrighted.

Answer questions 431 and 432 on the basis of the following passage.

(1) Theodore Roosevelt <u>were</u> born with asthma and poor eyesight. (2) Yet this sickly child later won fame as a political leader, Rough Rider, and hero of the common people. (3) To conquer his handicaps, Teddy trained in a gym and became a lightweight boxer at Harvard. (4) Out west, he hunted buffalo and ran a cattle ranch. (5) He was civil service reformer in the east and also a police commissioner. (6) He became President McKinley's Assistant Navy Secretary during the Spanish-American War. (7) Also, he led a charge of cavalry Rough Riders up San Juan Hill in Cuba. (8) After achieving fame, he became Governor of New York and went on to become the Vice-President.

431. Which of the following sentences represents the best revision of Part 5?
   a. Back east he became a civil service reformer and police commissioner.
   b. A civil service reformer and police commissioner was part of his job in the east.
   c. A civil service reformer and police commissioner were parts of his job in the east.
   d. His jobs of civil service reformer and police commissioner were his jobs in the east.

432. Which of the following should be used in place of the underlined verb in Part 1 of the above passage?
   a. will be
   b. are
   c. is
   d. was

Answer questions 433–435 on the basis of the following passage.

(1) Cuttlefish are very intriguing little animals. (2) The cuttlefish resembles a rather large squid and is, like the octopus, a member of the order of cephalopods. (3) Although they are not considered the most highly evolved of the cephalopods, cuttlefish are extremely intelligent. (4) _____. (5) While observing them, it is hard to tell who is doing the watching, you or the cuttlefish. (6) Since the eye of the cuttlefish is very similar in structure to the human eye, cuttlefish can give you the impression that you are looking into the eyes of a wizard who has metamorphosed himself into a squid with very human eyes.

(7) Cuttlefish are also highly mobile and fast creatures. (8) They come equipped with a small jet located just below the tentacles that can expel water to help them move. (9) For navigation, ribbons of flexible fin on each side of the body allow cuttlefish to hoover, move, stop, and start.

433. Which of the following sentences, if inserted into the blank numbered 4, would be most consistent with the paragraph's development and tone?
  a. Curious and friendly, cuttlefish tend, in the wild, to hover near a diver so they can get a good look, and in captivity, when a researcher slips a hand into the tanks, cuttlefish tend to grasp it with their tentacles in a hearty but gentle handshake.
  b. The cuttlefish can be cooked and eaten like its less tender relatives, the squid and octopus, but must still be tenderized before cooking in order not to be exceedingly chewy.
  c. Cuttlefish are hunted as food not only by many sea creatures, but also by people; they are delicious when properly cooked.
  d. Cuttlefish do not have an exoskeleton; instead their skin is covered with chromataphors.

434. Which of the following numbered parts should be revised to reduce its unnecessary repetition?
  a. Part 2
  b. Part 5
  c. Part 6
  d. Part 9

435. Which of the following changes should be made in the final sentence?
  a. Change *For* to *If*.
  b. Change *allow* to *allot*.
  c. Change *each* to *both*.
  d. Change *hoover* to *hover*.

SET 40 (Answers begin on page 147.)
Answer questions 436–438 on the basis of the following passage.

(1) As soon as she sat down on the airplane, Rachel almost began to regret telling the travel agent that she wanted an exotic and romantic vacation; after sifting through a stack of brochures, the agent and her decided the most exotic vacation she could afford was a week in Rio. (2) As the plane hurtled toward Rio de Janeiro, she read the information on Carnival that was in the pocket of the seat in front of hers. (3) The very definition made her shiver: "from the Latin carnavale, meaning a farewell to the flesh." (4) She was searching for excitement, but had no intention of bidding her skin good-bye. (5) "Carnival," the brochure informed her, originated in Europe in the Middle Ages and served as a break from the requirements of daily life and society. (6) Most of all, it allowed the hard-working and desperately poor serfs the opportunity to ridicule their wealthy and normally humorless masters." (7) Rachel, a middle manager in a computer firm, wasn't entirely sure whether she was a serf or a master. (8) Should she be making fun, or would others be mocking her? (9) She was strangely relieved when the plane landed, as though her fate were decided.

436. Which of the following changes needs to be made to the above passage?
   a. Part 6: Italicize *serfs*.
   b. Part 2: Insert *the* before *Carnival*.
   c. Part 3: Italicize *carnavale*.
   d. Part 9: Change *were* to *was*.

437. Which of the following numbered parts contains a nonstandard use of a pronoun?
   a. Part 1
   b. Part 5
   c. Part 7
   d. Part 8

438. Which of the following changes needs to be made to Part 5 of the above passage?
   a. Insert quotation marks before *originated*.
   b. Remove the comma after *her*.
   c. Remove the quotation marks after *Carnival*.
   d. Insert quotation marks after *society*.

Answer questions 439–441 on the basis of the following passage.

(1) A metaphor is a poetic device that deals with comparison. (2) It compares similar qualities of two dissimilar objects. (3) With a simple metaphor, one object becomes the other: *Love is a rose*. Although this doesn't sound like a particularly rich image, a metaphor can communicate so much about a particular image, that poets utilize them more than any other type of figurative language. (4) The reason for this is that a poet composes poetry to express emotional experiences. (5) <u>Succinctly</u>, what the poet imagines love to be may or

may not be our perception of love. (6) Therefore, the poet's job is to enable us to *experience* it and feel it the same way. (7) You should be able to nod in agreement and say, "Yes, that's it! (8) I understand precisely where this guy is coming from."

439. The tone of this passage is very formal; the last sentence is not. Which of the following would be more consistent with the tone of the passage?

a. This guy is right on.
b. I can relate to the poet's experience.
c. I know this feeling.
d. This poem gets right to the point.

440. Which of the following numbered parts contains a nonstandard use of a pronoun?

a. Part 3
b. Part 5
c. Part 6
d. Part 7

441. Which of the following adverbs should replace the underline word in Part 5 of the above passage?

a. Consequently
b. Normally
c. Occasionally
d. Originally

Answer questions 442–444 on the basis of the following passage.

(1) Light pollution a growing problem worldwide. (2) Like other forms of pollution, light pollution degrades the quality of the environment. (3) Where once it was possible to look up at the night sky and see thousands of twinkling stars in the inky blackness, one now sees little more than the yellow glare of urban sky glow. (4) When we lose the ability to connect visually with the vastness of the universe by looking up at the night sky, we lose our connection with something profoundly important to the human spirit, my sense of wonder.

442. Which of the endings to the following sentence would be the best concluding sentence for this passage?

The most serious damage done by light pollution is to our

a. artistic appreciation.
b. sense of physical well-being.
c. spiritual selves.
d. cultural advancement.

443. Which of the following numbered parts contains a nonstandard sentence?

a. Part 4
b. Part 3
c. Part 2
d. Part 1

444. Which of the following changes needs to be made to Part 4 of the passage?

a. Change *we* to *you*.
b. Change *my* to *our*.
c. Change *we* to *I*.
d. Change *my* to *his*.

SET 41 (Answers begin on page 148.)
Answer questions 445–447 on the basis of the following passage.

(1) Typically people think of genius, whether it manifests in Mozart composing symphonies at age five or Einstein's discovery of relativity, as having quality not just of the divine, but also of the eccentric. (2) People see genius as a "good" abnormality; moreover, they think of genius as a completely unpredictable abnormality. (3) Until recently, psychologists regarded the quirks of genius as too erratic to describe intelligibly; however, Anna Findley's groundbreaking study uncovers predictable patterns in the biographies of geniuses. (4) Despite the regularity of these patterns, they could still support the common belief that there is a kind of supernatural intervention in the lives of unusually talented men and women. (5) _____. (6) For example, Findley shows that all geniuses experience three intensely productive periods in their lives, one of which always occurs shortly before their deaths; this is true whether the genius lives to nineteen or ninety.

445. Which of the following sentences, if inserted in the blank numbered Part 5, would best focus the main idea of the passage?

a. These patterns are normal in the lives of all geniuses.

b. Eerily, the patterns themselves seem to be determined by predestination rather than mundane habit.

c. No matter how much scientific evidence the general public is presented with, people still like to think of genius as unexplainable.

d. Since people think of genius as a "good" abnormality, they do not really care what causes it.

446. Which of the following changes needs to be made to the passage?

a. Part 3: Change *too* to *to*.

b. Part 6: Change *geniuses* to *geniuses'*.

c. Part 1: Change *Mozart* to *Mozart's*.

d. Part 4: Change *there* to *their*.

447. Which of the following numbered parts contains a nonstandard use of a pronoun?

a. Part 4

b. Part 3

c. Part 6

d. Part 2

Answer questions 448–450 on the basis of the following passage.

(1) The English-language premiere of Samuel Beckett's play *Waiting for Godot* took place in London in August 1955. (2) *Godot* is an avant-garde play with only five characters (not including Mr. Godot, who never arrives) and a minimal setting—one rock and one bare tree. (3) The play has two acts, the second act repeating what little action occurs in the first with few changes: the tree, for instance, acquires one leaf. (4) Famously, the critic Vivian Mercer has described Godot as "a play in which nothing happens twice." (5) Opening night critics and playgoers, greeted the play with bafflement and derision. (6) Beckett's play managed to free the theater from the grasp of detailed naturalism. (7) The line, "Nothing happens, nobody comes, nobody goes. It's awful," was met by a loud rejoinder of "Hear! Hear!" from an audience member. (8) Despite the bad notices, director Peter Hall believed so passionately in the play that his fervor convinced the backers to refrain from closing the play at least until the Sunday reviews were published. (9) Harold Hobson's review in *The Sunday Times* managed to save the play, for Hobson had the vision to recognize the play for what history has proven it to be—a revolutionary moment in theater.

448. Which of the following editorial changes should be made in order to improve the focus and flow of the passage?
a. Reverse the order of Parts 6 and 7.
b. Part 3: remove the phrase, *the tree, for instance, acquires one leaf.*
c. Remove Part 9.
d. Remove Part 6.

449. Which of the following changes needs to be made to the passage?
a. Part 2: Italicize "Mr. Godot."
b. Part 2: Do not italicize "Godot."
c. Part 4: Italicize "Godot."
d. Part 9: Do not italicize "The Sunday Times."

450. From which of the following numbered parts should a comma be removed?
a. Part 3
b. Part 4
c. Part 5
d. Part 9

Answer questions 451–452 on the basis of the following passage.

(1) The Woodstock Music and Art Fair—better known to its participants and to history simply as "Woodstock"—should have been a colossal failure. (2) Just a month prior to its August 15, 1969 opening the fair's organizers were informed by the council of Wallkill, New York, that permission to hold the festival was withdrawn. (3) Amazingly, not only was a new site found, but word got out to the public of the fair's new location. (4) At the new site, fences that were supposed to facilitate ticket collection never materialized, all attempts at gathering tickets were abandoned. (5) Crowd estimates of 30,000 kept rising; by the end of the three days, some estimated the crowd at 500,000. (6) And then, on opening night, it began to rain. (7) Off and on, throughout all three days, huge summer storms rolled over the gathering. (8) In spite of these problems, most people think of Woodstock not only as a fond memory but as the defining moment for an entire generation.

451. In which of the following numbered parts should a comma be inserted?
- a. Part 1
- b. Part 2
- c. Part 3
- d. Part 4

452. Which of the following sentences is a run-on?
- a. Part 1
- b. Part 2
- c. Part 3
- d. Part 4

Answer questions 453–455 on the basis of the following passage.

(1) Whether or not you can accomplish a specific goal or meet a specific deadline depends first on how much time you need to get the job done. (2) What should you do when the demands of the job precede the time you have available. (3) The best approach is to correctly divide the project into smaller pieces. (4) Different goals will have to be divided in different ways, but one seemingly unrealistic goal can often be accomplished by working on several smaller, more reasonable goals.

453. Which of the following sentences has an error in the verb infinitive?
- a. Part 1
- b. Part 2
- c. Part 3
- d. Part 4

454. Which of the following words should replace the underlined word in Part 2 of the passage?
- a. exceed
- b. succeed
- c. supercede
- d. proceed

455. Which of the following sentences in the passage needs a question mark?

a. Part 2

b. Part 3

c. Part 1

d. Part 4

SET 42 (Answers begin on page 149.)

Answer questions 456 and 457 on the basis of the following passage.

(1) The Competitive Civil Service system is designed to give candidates fair and equal treatment and ensure that federal applicants are hired based on objective criteria. (2) Hiring has to be based solely on a candidate's knowledge, skills, and abilities (which you'll sometimes see abbreviated as KSA), and not on external factors such as race, religion, sex, and so on. (3) Whereas employers in the private sector can hire employees for subjective reasons, federal employers must be able to justify his decision with objective evidence that the candidate is qualified.

456. Which of the following sentences lacks parallelism?

a. Parts 2

b. Part 3

c. Parts 2 and 3

d. Part 1

457. Which of the following sentences has an error in pronoun agreement?

a. Part 1

b. Part 2

c. Part 3

d. Parts 2 and 3

Answer questions 458 and 459 on the basis of the following passage.

(1) A light rain was falling. (2) He drove home by his usual route. (3) It was a drive he had taken a thousand times; still, he did not know why, as he passed the park near their home, he should so suddenly and vividly picture the small pond that lay at the center of it. (4) In winter this pond was frozen over, and he had taken his daughter Abigail there when she was small and tried to teach her how to skate. (5) She hadn't been able to catch on, and so after two or three lessons Abigail and him had given up the idea. (6) Now there came into his mind an image of such clarity it caused him to draw in his breath sharply; an image of Abigail gliding toward him on her new Christmas skates, going much faster than she should have been.

458. Which of the following changes needs to be made to the passage?

a. Part 6: Change the semicolon to a colon.

b. Part 4: Remove the word "and."

c. Part 3: Change the semicolon to a comma.

d. Part 5: Change the comma to a semicolon

459. Which of the following changes needs to be made to the passage?

a. Part 4: Remove the comma after *over*.

b. Part 6: Replace *Christmas* with *Christmas'*.

c. Part 5: Change *him* to *he*.

d. Part 3: Replace *their* with *there*.

Answer questions 460–462 on the basis of the following passage.

(1) For years, Mt. Desert Island, particularly its major settlement, Bar Harbor, afforded summer homes for the wealthy. (2) Finally though, Bar Harbor has become a burgeoning arts community as well. (3) But, the best part of the island is the unspoiled forest land known as Acadia National Park. (4) Since the island sits on the boundary line between the temperate and sub-Arctic zones the island supports the flora and fauna of both zones as well as beach, inland, and alpine plants. (5) Lies in a major bird migration lane and is a resting spot for many birds. (6) The establishment of Acadia National Park in 1916 means that this natural monument will be preserved and that it will be available to all people, not just the wealthy. (7) Visitors to Acadia may receive nature instruction from the park naturalists as well as enjoy camping, hiking, cycling, and boating. (8) Or they may choose to spend time at the archeological museum learning about the Stone Age inhabitants of the island.

460. Which of the following sentences is a sentence fragment?
a. Part 5
b. Part 2
c. Part 4
d. Part 3

461. Which of the following adverbs should replace the words *Finally though* in Part 2?
a. Suddenly
b. Concurrently
c. Simultaneously
d. Recently

462. Which of the following changes needs to be made to Part 4?
a. Insert a comma after the word *zones*.
b. Delete the word *Because* at the beginning of the sentence.
c. Delete the comma after the word *inland*.
d. Add a question mark at the end of the sentence.

Answer questions 463 and 464 on the basis of the following passage.

(1) A smoke detector should be placed on each floor level of a home and outside each sleeping area. (2) A good site for a detector would be a hallway that runs between living spaces and bedrooms.

(3) Because of the "dead" air space that might be missed by turbulent hot air bouncing around above a fire, smoke detectors should be installed either at the ceiling at least four inches from the nearest wall, or high on a wall at least four, but no further than twelve, inches from the ceiling. (4) Detectors should not be mounted near windows, exterior doors, or other places where drafts might direct the smoke away from the unit. (5) Also, it should not be placed in kitchens and garages, where cooking and gas fumes are likely to set off false alarms.

463. Which of the following numbered parts contains a nonstandard use of a preposition?
a. Part 1
b. Part 3
c. Part 4
d. Part 5

464. In which of the following numbered parts should a pronoun be replaced with a different pronoun?

a. Part 2
b. Part 3
c. Part 5
d. Part 1

Answer questions 465–467 on the basis of the following passage.

(1) Heat exhaustion, generally characterized by clammy skin, fatigue, nausea, dizziness, profuse perspiration, and sometimes fainting, resulting from an inadequate intake of water and the loss of fluids. (2) First aid treatment for this condition includes having the victim lie down, raising the feet 8 to 12 inches, applying cool, wet cloths to the skin, and giving the victim sips of salt water (1 teaspoon per glass, half a glass every 15 minutes) over the period of an hour. (3) _____.

(4) Heat stroke is much more serious; it is an immediate life-threatening condition. (5) The characteristics of heat stroke are a high body temperature (which may reach 106 degrees F or more); a rapid pulse; hot, dry skin; and a blocked sweating mechanism. (6) Victims of this condition may be unconscious, and first aid measures should be directed at cooling the body quickly. (7) Heat stroke often occurs among poor people in urban areas. (8) The victim should be placed in a tub of cold water or repeatedly sponged with cool water until his or her temperature is lowered sufficiently. (9) Fans or air conditioners will also help with the cooling process. (10) Care should be taken, however, not to chill the victim too much once his or her temperature is below 102 degrees F.

465. Which of the following sentences, if inserted into the blank numbered Part 3 in the above passage, would best aid the transition of thought between the first and second paragraphs?

a. Heat exhaustion is a relatively unusual condition in northern climates.
b. The typical victims of heat stroke are the poor and elderly who cannot afford air conditioning even on the hottest days of summer.
c. Heat exhaustion is never fatal, although it can cause damage to internal organs if it strikes an elderly victim.
d. Air conditioning units, electric fans, and cool baths can lower the numbers of people who suffer heat stroke each year in the United States.

466. Which of the following numbered parts draws attention away from the main idea of the second paragraph of the passage?

a. Part 6
b. Part 7
c. Part 8
d. Part 10

467. Which of the following numbered parts contains a nonstandard sentence?

a. Part 1
b. Part 3
c. Part 5
d. Part 8

SET 43 (Answers begin on page 150.)
Answer questions 468 and 469 on the basis of the following passage.

(1) To test for carbon monoxide (CO) contamination, meters must be held head high. (2) Appliances should be operating for five to ten minutes before testing, a check must be made near all gas appliances and vents. (3) If vents are working properly, no CO emissions will enter the structure.

(4) If the meters register unsafe levels—above 10 parts per million (ppm)—all occupants should be evacuated and the source of the contamination investigated. (5) Occupants should be interviewed to ascertain the location of the CO detector (if any), the length of time the alarm has sounded, what the occupants been doing at the time of the alarm, and what electrical appliances were functioning. (6) Occupants should not re-enter the premises until the environment is deemed safe.

468. Which of the following numbered parts contains a nonstandard verb form?
a. Part 5
b. Part 3
c. Part 6
d. Part 2

469. Which of the following numbered parts contains a nonstandard sentence?
a. Part 6
b. Part 4
c. Part 2
d. Part 5

Answer questions 470 and 471 on the basis of the following passage.

(1) Glaciers consist of fallen snow that compresses over many years into large, thickened ice masses. (2) Most of the world's glacial ice is found in Antarctica and Greenland glaciers are found on nearly every continent, even Africa. (3) Presently, 10% of land area is covered with glaciers. (4) Glacial ice often appears blue because ice absorbs all other colors but reflects blue. (5) Almost 90% of an iceberg is below water; only about 10% shows above water. (6) What makes glaciers unique is their ability to move? (7) Due to sheer mass, glaciers flow like very slow rivers. (8) Some glaciers are as small as football fields, while others grow to be over a hundred kilometers long

470. Which of the following sentences is a run-on sentence?
a.   Part 4
b.   Part 3
c.   Part 2
d.   Part 1

471. Which of the following sentences contains an error in punctuation?
a.   Part 3
b.   Part 4
c.   Part 5
d.   Part 6

Answer question 472 on the basis of the following short description.

(1) Herbert was enjoying the cool, bright fall afternoon. (2) Walking down the street, red and yellow leaves crunched satisfyingly under his new school shoes.

472. Which of the following is the best revision of the description above?
a.   Herbert was enjoying the cool bright fall afternoon. Walking down the street red and yellow leaves crunched satisfyingly under his new school shoes.
b.   Herbert was enjoying the cool, bright fall afternoon. He was walking down the street, red and yellow leaves crunched satisfyingly under his new school shoes.
c.   Herbert was enjoying the cool, bright fall afternoon. Walking down the street, he crunched red and yellow leaves satisfyingly under his new school shoes.
d.   Herbert was enjoying the cool, bright fall afternoon. Walking down the street, red and yellow leaves were crunched satisfyingly under his new school shoes.

Answer questions 473–475 on the basis of the following passage.

(1) The building in which Howard Davis was to teach his undergraduate evening course, Interpretation of Poetry, was Renwick Hall, the General Sciences Building. (2) Markham Hall, which housed the English Department offices and classrooms, was to be closed all summer for renovation.

(3) Howard's classroom was in the basement. (4) The shadowy corridor that <u>led</u> back to it was lined with glass cases containing exhibits whose titles <u>read</u>, Small Mammals of North America, Birds of the Central United States, and Reptiles of the Desert Southwest. (5) The dusty specimens perched on little stands; <u>their</u> tiny claws gripped the smooth wood nervously. (6) A typewritten card, yellow with age, bearing the name of its genus and species. (7) The classroom itself was outfitted with a stainless steel sink, and behind the lectern loomed a dark-wood cabinet through whose glass doors one could see rows of jars, each holding what appeared to be an animal embryo floating in a murky liquid. (8) The classroom <u>wreaked</u> of formaldehyde.

473. Which of the following sentences, if inserted between Parts 6 and 7, would best fit the author's pattern of development in the second paragraph of the above passage?
a. Howard would be teaching Byron, Shelley, and Keats this term.
b. In the display case opposite Howard's classroom, a pocket gopher reared up on its hind legs, staring glassy-eyed into the open doorway.
c. Although Markham was at least twenty-five years younger than Renwick, the administration had chosen to renovate it rather than the aging, crumbling science building.
d. Genus and species are taxonomic categories.

474. Which of the following numbered parts contains a nonstandard sentence?
a. Part 1
b. Part 2
c. Part 6
d. Part 7

475. Which of the underlined words in the above paragraph needs to be replaced with its homonym?
a. led
b. their
c. read
d. wreaked

S·E·C·T·I·O·N

ESSAY QUESTIONS

The sets in this final section provide 26 essay-writing topics. These topics are representative of the kinds of writing prompts that you might find on an essay-writing test. As you plan and write practice essays, first choose the topics that are of interest to you or the topics that you know something about. When you begin to feel comfortable writing a 30-minute essay on a familiar subject, try writing about the topics that are less familiar—just to stretch your writing comfort zone.

Starting on page 150 of this book, in the Answers section, you will find a Scoring Guide. This guide shows a six-point scale, with 6 being an excellent essay and 1 being a poor essay. Guides like these are often used by teachers and evaluators of standardized writing tests to score your essay. You can use this guide to evaluate your own essays, or you can give the guide and your essay to a friend or teacher for comments. Often, a third party is much better at evaluating your writing than you are, yourself.

Also in the Answers section, you will find sample essays for the first six topics in this section (Sets 44-46). These essays will show you how the scoring guide is used to evaluate particular essays.

Generally, you should try for a score of 4 or above for your essays. If your essay falls below a score of 4, revise your work to see if you can raise it to a 5- or a 6-level essay, and show the new version to your evaluator.

SET 44 (Scoring guide on pages 150–151, sample essays start on page 151.)

Carefully read the essay-writing topics that follow. Choose one topic on which to write. Then, plan and write an essay that addresses all points in the topic you have chosen.

476. Should public school students be required to wear uniforms? Supporters argue that, among other things, uniforms improve discipline and build a strong sense of community and identity. On the other hand, opponents believe that uniforms limit students' freedom of expression and their development as individuals.

Write an essay in which you take a position on whether or not public school students should be required to wear uniforms to school. Be sure to support your position with logical arguments and specific examples.

477. Recently American students are said to have fallen behind in the sciences, and some educators believe it is because American teachers are conducting science classes ineffectively.

Write an essay in which you suggest ways science classes could be conducted so as to more effectively challenge high school and college students.

SET 45 (Scoring guide on pages 150–151, sample essays start on page 153.)

Make sure that your essays are well organized and that you support each central argument with concrete examples. Allow about 30 minutes for each essay.

478. In a review of Don DeLillo's novel *White Noise*, Jayne Anne Phillips writes that the characters are people "sleepwalking through a world where 'Coke is It!' and the TV is always on." On the other hand, television is said by some to have brought the world to people who would not have seen much of it otherwise. It has made possible a "global village."

Write an essay in which you express your opinion of the effect of television on individuals or on nations. Include specific details from personal experience to back up your assertions.

479. Bob Maynard has said that "Problems are opportunities in disguise."

Write an essay describing a time in your life when a problem became an opportunity. How did you transform the situation? Explain what you did to turn the problem into an opportunity, and explain how others can benefit from your experience.

SET 46 (Scoring guide on pages 150–151, sample essays start on page 158.)

When you write an essay under testing conditions, you should plan on using about the first one-fourth to one-third of the time you are allotted just for planning. Jot down notes about what you want to say about the topic, and then find a good way to organize your ideas.

480. In his play, *The Admirable Crighton*, J. M. Barrie wrote, "Courage is the thing. All goes if courage goes."

Write an essay about a time in your life when you had the courage to do something, face something difficult, or when you feel you fell short. What did you learn from the experience?

481. Some people say that writing can't be taught. Educators debate the subject every day, while the teachers in the trenches keep trying.

Write an essay in which you take a position about the matter. You may discuss any kind of writing, from basic composition to fiction. Be sure to back up your opinion with concrete examples and specific details.

SET 47 (Scoring guide on pages 150–151.)

The most important step in writing an essay is to read the topic carefully. Make sure you understand the question. If you have a choice of topics, choose the one you understand fully.

482. Dorothy Fosdick once said, "Fear is a basic emotion, part of our native equipment, and like all normal emotions has a positive function to perform. Comforting formulas for getting rid of anxiety may be just the wrong thing. Books about *peace of mind* can be bad medicine. To be afraid when one should be afraid is good sense."

Write an essay in which you express your agreement or disagreement with Fosdick's assertion. Support your opinion with specific examples.

483. In the past several years, many state governments have permitted gambling by actually sponsoring lotteries, to increase state revenues and keep taxes down. Proponents of gambling praise the huge revenues gambling generates. Opponents counter that gambling hurts those who can least afford it, and increased availability of gamblers leads to an increase in the number of gamblers who need treatment.

Write an essay in which you take a position on the issue of state-sponsored gambling. Be sure to support your view with logical arguments and specific examples.

SET 48 (Scoring guide on pages 150–151.)
Take just 30 minutes to plan and write your essay. This is good practice for writing under timed conditions, as you have to do in a test.

484. The Western view of human rights promotes individual rights. The Eastern view argues that the good of the whole country or people is more important than the rights of individuals.

Write an essay in which you take a position on this debate. The Western view would be that individuals always have the right to express their opinions. The Eastern view would hold that individual expression must sometimes be fettered in order to promote harmony in a given society. Be sure to support your discussion with specific examples and logical arguments.

485. Barbara Tuchman once noted, "Every successful revolution puts on in time the robe of the tyrant it has deposed."

Write an essay in which you either agree or disagree with her observation. Support your opinion with specific examples.

SET 49 (Scoring guide on pages 150–151.)
When planning your essay, use an outline, a brainstorming list, a topic map, or any other method that works for you to jot down your ideas and organize them logically.

486. Gossip is fun, but if it is malicious, it can be hurtful.

Have you ever been the victim of gossip? Have you ever passed on gossip that you later found was untrue? How do you think the victim of malicious gossip should react or respond? What advice would you give to such a victim?

487. In 1997, scientists in Scotland were successful in cloning a sheep. This event added to the debate over human cloning. Proponents of a ban on human cloning are concerned about issues such as genetic selection. Opponents of a ban point out that cloning could lead to significant medical advances.

Write an essay in which you take a position on the issue of human cloning. Be sure to support your view with logical arguments and specific examples.

SET 50 (Scoring guide on pages 150–151.)
When you write, make sure the first paragraph of your essay includes a thesis statement, a sentence that states the main idea of your essay.

488. Law enforcement agencies use a tool called profiling in certain situations. Profiling is the practice of outlining the looks and behavior of the type of person who is more likely than others to commit a particular crime. For example, if a person buys an airline ticket with cash, travels with no luggage, and returns the same day, they fit the profile for a drug courier. Opponents of profiling argue that it has the potential to unfairly target citizens based on their appearance. Proponents argue that law enforcement must take such shortcuts in order to effectively fight crime.

Write an essay in which you take a position on this debate. Be sure to use logical reasoning and be sure to support your view with specific examples.

489. Is it ever all right to lie? Some people say that "little white lies" are acceptable to spare someone else's feelings. Other people believe it is never right to lie, that telling a few little lies leads to telling more and bigger lies.

Which position do you hold? Is it possible to never lie? Is it possible to tell just the right amount of lies? Use examples to illustrate your position.

SET 51 (Scoring guide on pages 150–151.)
There's no specific number of paragraphs you have to have in an essay, but it would be difficult, to write a good essay on any topic in fewer than three paragraphs. Most good essays will have four to seven paragraphs.

490. The United States owes the United Nations several million dollars in back-dues and other fees. Opponents of paying this debt point to an inefficient bureaucracy at the United Nations and the tendency of the United Nations to support positions that are not in the United States' best interests. Proponents of paying this debt highlight a growing tendency toward internationalism and the fact that the United States depends on the United Nations for support.

Write an essay outlining why the United States should pay its United Nations debt or why it should not. Support your position with examples and logical arguments.

491. As juvenile crime increases, so do the calls for stricter punishments for juvenile offenders. One suggestion is to lower the age at which a juvenile may be tried as an adult. Supporters of this view believe that young people are committing crimes at younger and younger ages, and the crimes they are committing are becoming more and more heinous. Opponents of this view point to the success of juvenile crime prevention programs, such as teen centers and midnight basketball.

Write an essay in which you either defend or criticize the suggestion that juvenile offenders should be charged as adults at younger ages. Include examples and logical reasoning to support your position.

SET 52 (Scoring guide on pages 150–151.)
The essays in this set and the next few contain more personal topics—ones that ask you to reflect on a specific event in your life or on your personality.

492. Phyliss Bottome has said, "There are two ways of meeting difficulties. You alter the difficulties or you alter yourself to meet them."

Write about a time in which you attempted to alter a difficult situation, or decided to alter yourself. Were you successful? Are you pleased with the choice you made? Whichever you chose to alter, would it have been easier to alter the other? Would it have been better?

493. Bella Lewitzky once said, "To move freely you must be deeply rooted."

Write an essay in which you first state what you interpret this statement to mean (there is no right or wrong interpretation), then (using your own interpretation) agree or disagree with it. Support your opinion with specific examples and logical reasoning.

SET 53 (Scoring guide on pages 150–151.)
Each body paragraph of your essay should have a topic sentence that forecasts the main idea of that paragraph. Make sure your topic sentences are connected to your thesis statement in order to write a unified essay.

494. Most people have faced a situation—perhaps in a class, an organization, or just with a group of friends—in which they held a strong, but unpopular, opinion.

Write about a time when you were in this circumstance. Did you speak up? Did you keep quiet? Why do you think you made the choice you did?

495. Do you consider yourself adventurous, a risk-taker?

Write about a time in which you contemplated an undertaking which others considered dangerous. Did you do it? Why? If you did not do it, why not? Do you have regrets? The danger involved need not have been physical, although it could have been.

SET 54 (Scoring guide on pages 150–151.)
It's always important to explain yourself fully. How will the reader understand the event you're describing if you don't "show all"? In both personal and persuasive writing, it's important to include lots of details, images, and explanations to support your main idea.

496. Nadine Stair said, "If I had my life to live over again, I'd dare to make more mistakes next time."

Write an essay in which you agree or disagree with this assessment, using your own life as a touchstone. Why do you agree or disagree? How might your life have been different if you had dared to make more mistakes?

497. In the 1960s and 1970s, women were demanding the right to attend previously all-male educational institutions. By the 1990s, having won that right, some women are now reconsidering. Citing studies that indicate girls perform better in all-girl schools than in coed schools, some women are calling for the establishment of single-sex educational institutions.

Write an essay in which you take a position on the issue of single-sex schools. Be sure to include specific examples and solid reasoning in your opinion.

SET 55 (Scoring guide on pages 150–151.)
Often the best way to organize a personal essay is chronologically, in time order. But you should still make sure you have a thesis statement that responds to the question, and that your whole essay is related to your thesis statement.

498. Susanne Curchod Necker said, "Worship your heroes from afar; contact withers them."

Do you agree? Write about a time when you made contact with a hero. Were you disappointed with the experience or not? Or, perhaps someone once thought of you as a hero. Did they feel the same way after they got close to you? Did closeness make the relationship better or worse?

499. Most of us have been in a situation, perhaps at work or at school, in which we felt we were being treated unfairly.

Write about a time when you were treated unfairly. How did you react? What did you do or say about the treatment? If you had it to do over again, would you do something differently?

SET 56 (Scoring guide on pages 150–151.)
Whether you're writing a personal essay or a persuasive one, make sure you stick to the topic you are given.

500. An old cliché says, "You can't fight city hall."

Do you believe this is true? What advice would you give someone who wanted to convince a city council that a stoplight should be installed at a particular corner? Perhaps you can write about a time in which you tried to change or enact a law, or perhaps a regulation at school or work. Were you successful? Why or why not?

501. Advances in genetic testing now allow scientists to identify people whose genetic background makes them greater risks for certain diseases. A genetic predisposition to a certain disease, however, does not guarantee that a patient will contract that disease. Environmental factors, such as diet, exercise, and smoking also play a role. Insurance companies want to have access to genetic information in order to help keep their costs down. Opponents feel that insurance companies will misuse such information, by unfairly denying people coverage.

Write an essay in which you take a position on providing genetic testing information to insurance companies. Be sure to support your argument with specific examples and logical reasoning.

ANSWERS

SECTION 1: MECHANICS

SET 1 (Page 8)

1. **b.** A title, such as *Dr.*, takes a capital.
2. **d.** Nationalities and languages take capitals.
3. **a.** *Jr.* is a kind of title and therefore takes a capital.
4. **b.** The first letter of a direct quotation takes a capital.
5. **e.** Capitalization is correct.
6. **a.** All words in the proper name of a place take capitals.
7. **b.** Proper names take capitals.
8. **c.** Movie titles are capitalized.

SET 2 (Page 9)

9. **d.** There should be quotation marks before the word *My* to set off the dialogue.
10. **d.** Commas set off nonrestrictive appositives, phrases that say the same thing as the previous phrase in different words. (Place a comma after *Roy*.)
11. **a.** A colon can go before a list (after the word *foods*).
12. **a.** A semicolon can be used to separate two main clauses, which could each stand alone as complete sentences.
13. **c.** A dash can be used to set off a parenthetical element, for emphasis. (Place another dash after the word *woman*.)
14. **a.** The possessive *Jack's* takes an apostrophe.

15. e. This sentence is punctuated correctly.

16. b. Commas set off parenthetical elements and always go inside the quotation marks in a line of dialogue (after the word *wonder*).

17. d. Commas set off a word or phrase that describes the subject but does not alter the meaning of the entire sentence (after *Bailey*).

18. c. A semicolon can be used to separate two main clauses, which could each stand alone as complete sentences. (Place the semicolon after the word *baseball*.)

SET 3 (Page 10)

19. b. The comma separates the main clause from the long, descriptive subordinate clause.

20. d. The semicolon can be used to separate two main clauses, which could each stand alone as complete sentences.

21. a. The quotation is a question, and the tag *asked Samantha* ends the sentence.

22. e. The sentence is punctuated correctly.

23. b. The word *dog's* is possessive and needs an apostrophe; the comma is optional.

24. e. The sentence does not require any punctuation other than the period at the end.

25. c. This is a declarative sentence; it asks an indirect question, so a question mark should not be used. Also, the comma is unnecessary.

26. e. The sentence is punctuated correctly.

27. a. The phrase *a virus* is a nonessential element in the sentence and needs to be set off with commas.

28. d. Commas separate dates and addresses.

SET 4 (Page 11)

29. a. *Spring* should not be capitalized.

30. c. There should not be an apostrophe after the word *boys*.

31. a. The comma is unnecessary and should be deleted.

32. b. *Senator* should be capitalized because it refers to a particular senator.

33. c. *Cape Cod* is a proper noun, and both words should be capitalized.

34. a. Since this is a declarative sentence, the question mark should be replaced with a period.

35. b. *Uncle* is not used as a proper noun and should not be capitalized.

36. a. *Grandma* is used as a proper name and should be capitalized.

37. b. A colon should not be used between a verb and its objects.

38. a. There should be an apostrophe in the word *else's*, which is possessive.

39. c. The commas are missing from this series of adjectives.

40. b. The quotation mark should appear on the outside of the exclamation point: "*Don't run!*"

41. c. *Polio* and *smallpox* should not be capitalized. Diseases are not capitalized unless a proper noun is part of the name.

42. a. *Ocean* should be capitalized.

43. c. To set off the dialogue, there should be quotation marks before the word *I'll*.

44. c. *Mayor* should not be capitalized because it does not refer to a particular mayor.

45. b. A semicolon is not used between a dependent and an independent clause. Use a comma.

46. b. *Veterinarian* is not a proper noun and should not be capitalized.

47. c. The word *Why*, which begins the quotation, should be capitalized.

48. b. *World War* is a proper noun and should be capitalized.

49. a. The phrase *like many other viruses* should be set off by commas because it is a nonessential element in the sentence.

50. a. *Industrial Revolution* should be capitalized.

51. a. The commas in this sentence should be deleted. Commas are not used in a series when the series is already linked by conjunctions.

52. a. The names of centuries are not capitalized.

53. c. This sentence asks a question and should end with a question mark.

SET 5 (Page 13)

54. c. Commas are used to set off a word or phrase that describes the subject but does not alter the meaning of the entire sentence.

55. e. The dash is used to set off parenthetical elements, for emphasis.

56. a. The comma is used after an introductory element.

57. b. The comma separates the main clause from the descriptive subordinate clause.

58. c. Titles take capitals.

59. d. First word of salutations, titles, and proper names all take capitals; a colon follows the salutation in a business letter.

60. d. Commas set off parenthetical elements

61. a. A comma goes before *and* when *and* links two main clauses.

SECTION 2: SENTENCE STRUCTURE

SET 6 (page 17)

62. d. *Although* means "despite the fact that" or "even though." Even though strip mining is cheap, it is harmful. The other choices do not convey this meaning.

63. a. *Therefore* best completes the sentence's meaning; it creates a cause and effect relationship between Yori's cold (the cause) and Yori's decision not to attend the movie that night (the effect).

64. b. *While* suggests that two things are happening simultaneously; it is the only logical choice. Choice a implies that Julia could control when the bus would arrive. Choices c and d are unclear.

65. c. The sentence requires a condition—the mother likes rock music on one condition: low volume. Choice a can be ruled out because rock music is not always played at a low volume. Choices b and d result in unclear sentences.

66. a. *However* indicates an impending contradiction; it is the best choice because the two clauses compare tastes. In this case, the comparison contrasts Joelle's preference to Chelsea's.

67. d. If you rearrange the sentence, it would read: If you sign up now, you will receive low interest rates **and** a free gift. *In addition* means *and*; it is the best choice. Choices a and b result in an awkward construction. Choice c is illogical.

68. b. The two clauses make a reference to time—more specifically, to two different times. Choice b is the only logical response.

69. **d.** The dog's ears are covered because he is afraid of thunder; one is the effect of the other. *Consequently* means *following as an effect* or *as a result*. This is the best choice.

70. **a.** This sentence speculates that quilts were made *from* fabrics taken *from* somewhere. Only *from* completes this idea.

71. **d.** This is the only choice that results in a complete and logical sentence. Choice **a** is illogical; choices **b** and **c** result in sentence fragments.

72. **d.** The conditional tense, *would have heard*, is the only one that logically fits with the second clause of the sentence.

73. **c.** The Beatles songs specifically named were pulled from a pool of titles. Only *Among* suggests the existence of many other things, in this case songs.

SET 7 (Page 18)

74. **c.** *Even though* is the most logical subordinating phrase, showing a contrast. The other choices are not only illogical but ungrammatical.

75. **b.** In this choice, the subordinate clause makes sense. Choice **b** is also the least wordy of the choices. In choices **a** and **d**, the subordinators are illogical. Choice **c** contains a misplaced modifier (Plato believed; Plato's idea could not believe.)

76. **a.** The word *despite* establishes a logical connection between the main and subordinate clauses. *Whereupon* and *so that* (choices **b** and **c**) make no sense. Choice **d** is both illogical and ungrammatical.

77. **c.** The subordinator *because* in choice **c** establishes the logical causal relationship between subordinate and main clause;

choices **a** and **b** do not make sense. Choice **d** has faulty construction.

78. **b.** *Whereas* (in choice **b**) is the logical subordinator, establishing contrast. The other answer choices make no sense.

79. **b.** The subordinators *after* (choice **a**), *whereupon* (choice **c**), and *unless* (choice **d**) do not make sense. Although the word *but* (choice **b**) can be used as a coordinating conjunction, here it is a subordinator, logically connecting subordinate and main clause.

80. **c.** The subordinator *although* shows a logical contrasting relationship between subordinate and main clause. The other choices do not make sense.

81. **b.** The subordinator *so* (choice **b**) establishes the correct causal relationship between main and subordinate clause. The other subordinators do not point to cause.

82. **d.** The subordinator *yet* establishes a contrasting relationship between the main and subordinate clauses. The other choices do not establish a logical relationship.

83. **a.** The subordinator *whereas* (choice **a**) correctly establishes a contrast between subordinate and main clause. The other choices point to an illogical causal relationship.

84. **c.** Choice **a** contains a misplaced modifier. Choice **b** is a run-on sentence. Choice **d** establishes a faulty causal relationship between main and subordinate clauses. Choice **c** correctly states a simple fact.

SET 8 (Page 21)

85. c. The conjunction *but* sets the reader up for a contrast or opposite: TV passive . . . *(but)* computer game active.

86. b. The conjunction *so* indicates a causal relationship: *Socrates taught* [something obviously controversial], . . . *so he was . . . both loved and . . . . hated.* Choice **c** is incorrect because it has a misplaced modifier.

87. a. The conjunction *for* in this sentence means *because* and prepares the reader for a logical causal relationship. Choice **d** is a run-on sentence.

88. a. The conjunction *so* indicates that there is a causal relationship between the two main clauses.

89. d. The conjunction *yet* prepares the reader for a contrast: *respected, yet . . . imprisoned.* Choice **b** is wrong because it is unclear.

90. c. In this sentence, the conjunction *for* means *because* and prepares the reader a logical causal relationship: *new shoes . . . (for) Donnie will be upset if . . . flip-flops.*

91. c. The conjunction *so* indicates a logical causal relationship between the first main clause and the second: *loaded with money, (so) she can afford.*

92. b. The conjunction *but* sets the reader up for an opposite or contrast: *it is possible . . . (but) unlikely.* Choices **c** and **d** make no sense.

93. c. The word *Unless* sets up the causal relationship between the two clauses in the sentence. The other choices are illogical.

94. a. The subordinating conjunction *Although* signals an impending contradiction; it makes the most sense. The other choices do not make sense.

95. d. The subordinator *but* contrasts the main clause and subordinate clause in a logical way. Choices **a**, **b**, and **c** do not make sense.

96. d. Choice **d** is the most economical of the choices and makes the most sense.

SET 9 (Page 24)

97. d. *Because* establishes the causal relationship between the man's tardiness and everyone's worry.

98. b. The transitional word *whereas* correctly establishes a contrast between the speaker's opinion of Earl and everyone else's opinion.

99. c. The transitional word *although* correctly establishes a contrast between Maya's I.Q. and her inability to read, which supposedly accompanies intelligence.

100. c. The conjunctive adverb *therefore* establishes the causal relationship between the reoccurrence of tornadoes and the area's name.

101. a. The transitional word *however* correctly establishes a contrast between the owl's predatory appearance and its docile nature.

102. a. The transitional word *furthermore* correctly indicates the addition of one unpleasant trait to another. Choice **d** is wrong because not all crooks have unpleasant personalities.

103. a. The conjunction *but* means *on the contrary*, and indicates that the two negatives in the first main clause will be followed by their opposite or opposites in the second: *never had food fights or cut classes . . . (but) did* smoke. Choice **b** makes an illogical connection. Choice **d** is unclear.

104. c. The conjunction *but* indicates that the first main clause will be followed by something that indicates an opposite or contrast: must be frightening . . . (*but*) cannot be as frightening as.

105. d. The conjunction *so* correctly indicates causality: the speaker leaves the light on because of his or her fear of the dark. Choice **a** indicates causality but is ungrammatical. Choice **c** is unclear.

106. b. The conjunction *yet* prepares the reader for a contrast: is not usually . . . (*yet*) it can. Choice **c** is unclear.

107. d. The conjunction *and* in this sentence indicates *also*. Choice **a** is wrong because it is a sentence fragment. Choice **b** makes no sense; choice **c** prepares the reader for a contrast but fails to deliver: *narcolepsy is* occurs in both main clauses.

108. b. The conjunction *yet* prepares the reader for a contrast: much interest throughout the ages . . . (*yet*) scientific study . . . is . . . new. Choices **a** and **c** are incomplete sentences.

SET 10 (Page 26)

109. a. Correct as is. This sentence requires the same form (parallelism) between the verbs *meet* and *have*, and choice **a** is the only sentence that does this (meeting and having).

110. c. This choice is the only one that does not contain repetition or wordiness. In choices **a** and **d**, the words *wide*, *variety*, and *different* mean the same thing, and in choice **e** *many* and *numerous* mean the same thing.

111. b. This choice is correctly subordinated and is logical.

112. a. Correct as is. This is the only choice that does not have faulty subordination. The first part of the sentence is an independent clause; the second part is a dependent clause. Choice **a** is correct because the dependent clause is correctly introduced by the relative pronoun *which*.

113. e. This is the only choice that does not contain repetition or wordiness. In choices **a**, **c**, and **d**, *well-known*, *prominent*, *famous* and *renown* mean the same thing; in choice **b**, a painter obviously lived and painted.

114. c. This choice is constructed so that the sentence is logical and unambiguous. The opening phrase *Having stopped twice to get gas* should be completed by a noun that indicates who stopped for gas.

115. a. Correct as is. This is the only choice that does not contain repetition or wordiness. In choice **b**, *cautious* and *careful* mean the same thing; in choice **c**, *guarding* and *protecting* mean the same thing; and in choice **d**, *workers* and *employees* are the same thing.

116. d. The word *beside* means at the side of; the word *besides* means other than or together with.

117. d. The comparison in this sentence between the U.S. and Europe requires *as well as*. Choice **d** does this while at the same time creating a sentence that is clear and logical.

118. a. Correct as is. A comma is needed before a coordinating conjunction and after a subordinating clause; choice **a** is the only one that does both.

119. d. In this complex sentence, **d** is the only choice that results in a complete sentence. The other choices are sentence fragments.

SET 11 (Page 29)

120. b. This is the only choice in which the sentence construction is clear and unambiguous. In choices **a** and **c**, the sentence reads as though the ingredients were making the torte. In choice **e**, no one is making the torte. Choice **d** is incorrect because there is a shift in tense from present (*making*) to past perfect (*should have used*).

121. a. Correct as is. This sentence requires that the comparison between culture and biology be logical and clear. Choice **b** is wrong because the use of the preposition *with* does not observe standard usage conventions. The phrase *somewhat better* in choice **c** makes no sense. Choices **d** and **e** result in an unclear comparison.

122. e. This is the only choice that does not contain excessive wordiness or a redundancy. In choice **a**, the phrase *the fifth of five* is redundant. Choices **b**, **c**, and **d** also repeats *five* and *fifth*.

123. e. The opening phrase, *An American poet of the nineteenth century*, should modify a noun that identifies the poet. Only choice **e** does this. In choices **a**, **b**, and **c**, either *collection* or *Leaves of Grass* is illogically credited with being the poet. Choice **d** is incorrect because the subject of the resulting dependent clause, *poems*, would not agree with its verb, *celebrates*.

124. d. Choice **d** is correctly punctuated with a semicolon between two independent clauses, and there is no shift in person. Choices **a**, **b**, and **e** are incorrect because the sentence shifts from the first person (*We*) to the second person (*you*). Choice **c** uses a semicolon when no punctuation is necessary.

125. b. In this sentence *Contrary to*, which means a viewpoint that is opposite to or in conflict with another viewpoint, is used correctly. In choice **a**, *in* is inappropriately used with opposite. Similarly, choices **c**, **d**, and **e** do not use standard phrasing.

126. a. Correct as is. Choices **b** and **e** are wordy while choices **c** and **d** are awkward.

127. c. Choices **a**, **b** and **e** are awkward and wordy. Choice **d** is unclear and ambiguous; the use of the preposition *to* distorts the meaning of the sentence.

128. d. This choice is clear, logical, and unambiguous and does not use extraneous words. Choice **a** is redundant: *until the time when*. Choice **b** is also redundant (*since when*) and uses extraneous words. The redundancy in choice **c** is *to kill and stop*. In choice **e**, the phrase *up to when* is awkward, and the word *its* has an unclear referent.

129. a. When constructing sentences, unnecessary shifts in verb tenses should be avoided. Choice **a** is best because all three verbs in the sentence indicate that the action occurred in the past (*had been covering, became,* and *was called*). In choice **b**, there is a shift to the present (*becomes*). Choice **c** begins in the present (*is covering, becomes*), then shifts to the past (*called*). Choice **d** makes two tense shifts, and choice **e** shifts once, from present to past tense.

130. d. This is the only choice that is both grammatically and logically correct. Choice **a** has a shift in construction; there are two subjects that mean the same thing (*Lee Iacocca* and *he*). Choice **b** has a modifier problem; the sentence implies that Lee Iacocca worked his way to the top because he was the son of immigrants. Choice **c**, though constructed differently, results in the same faulty logic. Choice **e** creates faulty subordination.

131. e. The correct punctuation between two independent clauses is a semicolon. Choice **a** is wrong because it creates a comma splice. Choice **c** creates a sentence fragment. Choices **b** and **d** create faulty subordination.

132. b. This is the correct choice because it is the only one that is a complete sentence.

133. e. This is the correct choice because the sentence is complete, logical, and unambiguous.

134. b. This is the only choice that is logical and unambiguous.

SET 12 (Page 31)

135. c. This is a sentence fragment.

136. a. The word *going* needs to be deleted.

137. d. There are no errors.

138. b. This is a run-on sentence.

139. c. The modifier *last fall* is misplaced. A modifier should be nearest to the subject or action that it modifies; in this case, that action is *visited*, not *lived*. The sentence should read: *Last fall we visited the house where President George Washington lived.*

140. d. There are no errors.

141. c. The word *unless* does not logically connect the independent clauses. The sentence needs a word that indicates contrast, because what Joshua does and what Joshua expects are two opposite things; the coordinating conjunction *but* should replace *unless*.

142. a. This is a run-on sentence.

143. b. This is a sentence fragment.

144. d. There are no errors.

145. d. There are no errors.

146. b. The word *that* is unnecessary; two independent clauses use a comma and a coordinating conjunction.

SET 13 (Page 33)

147. a. The other choices are unclear because they are awkwardly constructed, obscuring who intends to set the fire.

148. a. Answers **b** and **c** are sentence fragments. Answer **d** represents confused sentence structure as well as lack of agreement between subject and verb.

149. c. The other choices contain unnecessary shifts in person: from *people* to *their* and *we* in answer **a**, to *your* and *one* in answer **b**, and to *our* and *they* in answer **d**.

150. a. This is the only choice that is clear and logical. It has no misplaced modifiers, and it has no shifts in verb tense. Choices **b** and **d** have misplaced modifiers and result in unclear sentences; choice **c** has an unnecessary shift from past to present tense.

151. b. This is the only choice that does not have a misplaced modifier. Because Miles Johnson is the sharpshooter, his name should be placed immediately after the introductory phrase—which rules out choices **a** and **c**. Choice **d** is awkwardly constructed and unclear.

152. c. This is the only choice that is clear and logical. Choice **a** reads as though the eyes are in the third or fourth grade. Choices **b** and **d** are unclear.

153. c. Choice **c** creates a clear comparison. It is the only choice that is clear and logical.

Section 3: Agreement

SET 14 (Page 37)

154. a. The verb is formed incorrectly; *must of missed* should be replaced by *must have missed*.

155. b. This is an error in subject-verb agreement. The subject, *television shows*, is plural and requires a plural verb form. In this case, the correct form is *transcend*, not the singular form *transcends*.

156. b. The error is grammatical; there is no subject-verb agreement in this sentence. The subject *Each* is singular and requires a singular verb form in this situation, the correct form is *has had*.

157. a. This is an error in agreement. The singular noun *one* requires the singular verb *is*. When the subject (in this case *one*) follows the verb, as in a sentence beginning with *here* or *there*, be careful to determine the subject. In this sentence, the subject is not the plural noun *books*.

158. d. This sentence has an illogical shift in verb tense. The sentence should read: *he realized that he had missed the bus.*

159. d. In this sentence there is faulty parallelism. The word *asking* should be replaced by the verb *asked*. This sentence is in the past tense so the two verbs *asked* and *phoned* should be parallel.

160. d. The use of the present participle *creating* results in a sentence with faulty parallelism. A form of the verb *create* should be parallel with the preceding verb *became*, which is in the past tense. The word *creating* should be replaced by *created*.

161. b. There is no subject-verb agreement in this sentence. The singular collective noun *staff* requires a singular verb form. Therefore, the plural form *deserve* should be replaced with the singular *deserves*.

162. d. This sentence has faulty parallelism. There are three items in a series in this sentence: *build homes, find water,* and *learn to understand the blessings*. To make these three items parallel, the word *to* should be deleted in the underlined portion represented by choice **d**.

163. d. There is no subject-verb agreement in the sentence. The subject of the second independent clause is *filter*, a singular noun. Therefore, the singular form of the verb should be used. The verb *reduce* should be replaced by the verb *reduces*.

164. b. This sentence has a problem with subject-verb agreement. The two subjects of the sentence, *chief executive officer* and *chairman of the board*, require a plural verb. In this case, the singular form *agrees* should be replaced by the plural form *agree*.

165. b. The error is in verb formation. The sentence requires the past tense of the verb *begin*. To correct this error, the past participle *begun* should be replaced with the past tense *began*.

SET 15 (Page 39)

166. c. The sentence requires a verb in the past tense.

167. d. The sentence requires a verb in the past tense.

168. d. The appropriate tense for this verb is the present tense.

169. b. The verbal form *been seeing* fits with the verb *have*.

170. c. The infinitive form of the verb, *rescue*, goes with *to* in the sentence.

171. a. This is a command; the subject of the sentence is understood (*You put*).

172. d. The verb *was* agrees with its subject, *problem*, and is in the past tense.

173. c. Since the action takes places in the past, the only correct choice is the past perfect *had fallen*.

174. b. This is the only choice that is in agreement with the plural subject *people*.

175. c. The correct verb form is the past tense *flung*.

176. b. The verb *are* agrees with the plural noun *ways*.

177. a. The singular verb *gets* agrees with the singular noun *noise*.

SET 16 (Page 40)

178. d. A plural subject takes a plural verb; since the subject *words* is plural, the verb *to be carved* must also be plural.

179. a. Correct as is. There are two possible errors in this sentence: one is subject/verb agreement and the other is the use of the words *between* and *among*. *Between* is used to compare two things; *among* is used to compare more than two things. Since the subject *relationship* is singular, the verb *to determine* must also be singular. Only choice **a** makes the comparison between two things and uses the singular verb *determines*.

180. d. The three underlined elements make a coordinated series; to clearly express their relationship to each other, they need to abide by one consistent grammatical construction. In choice **a**, the verb *must generate* breaks the parallelism. In choice **b**, the word *for* breaks the parallelism. In choice **c**, the series changes construction, adopting a different type of parallel construction; however, the third element, soil conservation, does not use a present participle verb before it. It breaks the parallelism. In choice **e**, none of the three elements are parallel.

181. b. The two underlined elements make a coordinated pair; they need to abide by one grammatical construction. Only in choice **b** are both verbs in their infinitive form.

182. c. In choice **c**, the tense of *to ring* and *to write* agree; there is no shift in tense.

183. d. Choice **d** is best because it is written in the active voice.

184. e. Choice **a** is ambiguous: Is everyone submitting to the council? Choices **b**, **c**, and **d** make an illogical shift in verb tense.

185. b. The second clause of this sentence requires a parallel construction. Choice **b** is the only one in which all four elements use the same grammatical construction, a verb in the present tense followed by a noun.

186. **b.** This is the best answer because there are no shifts in verb tense. For the sentence to be logical, all the verbs should remain in the past tense.

187. **d.** *To ensure* means to make certain; *to assure* means to cause a feeling of certainty. The Senator wants his constituents to feel secure; he is not actually securing the money by putting it in a vault. Choice e is redundant; the verbs *to assure* and *to promise* mean the same thing.

188. **e.** Conscience is a moral awareness; conscious is a physical awareness. Josh was awake and physically aware of his environment. Choices a and b use the wrong word to describe Josh's condition. In choice d, it seems the operation was given a local anesthetic, not Josh.

SET 17 (Page 42)

189. **b.** The correct verb form is *rose*.

190. **b.** There is no subject-verb agreement. The verb should be plural because the subject, *words*, is plural.

191. **b.** The verb is used incorrectly. The correct usage is *should have been*.

192. **c.** The verb in this sentence has been incorrectly formed; it should be *drank*, not *drunk*.

193. **b.** There is no subject-verb agreement. The verb should be singular because the subject, *oldest*, is singular.

194. **a.** The sentence makes an illogical shift in tense—from the present to the past tense.

195. **b.** There is no subject-verb agreement. The verb should be plural because the subject, *photographs*, is plural.

196. **d.** There are no errors.

197. **b.** The correct verb form is *has broken*.

198. **a.** The correct verb form is *rang*.

199. **b.** The sentence makes an illogical shift in tense—from the past to the present tense.

200. **b.** There is no subject-verb agreement. The verb should be singular because the subject, *one* (not *boys*), is singular.

201. **c.** The correct verb form is *has worn*.

202. **a.** This sentence makes an illogical shift in tense—from the past to the present tense.

SET 18 (Page 43)

203. **a.** The verbs *got* and *took* agree in tense.

204. **d.** The verbs *liked* and *got* agree in tense.

205. **a.** *Became* and *eating* are the correct forms of the verbs.

206. **a.** This is a complete sentence; the others are fragments.

207. **d.** This is a complete sentence; the others are fragments.

208. **b.** This is a complete sentence; c and d are fragments; in choice a the verb does not agree in number with its subject, *one*.

209. **b.** This is a complete sentence; the others are fragments.

210. **a.** The comparison between the speaker's and his or her sister's taste for fish is clearest in this sentence. In choice b, the speaker likes his/her sister better than fish. Choice c does not make sense. Choice d has an ambiguous pronoun: *it* probably refers to fish, but who can tell?

211. **a.** In choice b, the cat seems to be renting the room. In choice c, it's unclear whether *he* refers to the cat or to Mr. Morris; answer d implies that Mr. Morris rented himself a room.

212. d. In this sentence, the verb tense between the independent clause and the subordinating clause agree. In choice **a**, the lack of agreement in tense makes the sentence unclear as to time; choice **b** doesn't make it clear who ate the popcorn; choice **c** implies that the popcorn watched the movie.

SET 19 (Page 44)

213. e. Because there are no grammatical, idiomatic, logical, or structural errors in this sentence, **e** is the best answer.

214. a. *Their* should be replaced with the contraction *They're*, meaning *They are*.

215. d. This is a grammatical error. The contraction *it's* (meaning *it is*) should be replaced by the possessive pronoun *its*.

216. e. Because there are no grammatical errors in this sentence, the best answer is choice **e**.

217. e. Because there are no grammatical errors in this sentence, choice **e** is the best answer.

218. a. This is an error of agreement. The singular pronoun *it* does not agree with the plural noun *mollusks*. In this sentence *it* should be replaced by the plural pronoun *they*.

219. c. This is an error in agreement. The singular pronoun *him* does not agree with its antecedent, the plural noun *people*. The word *him* should be replaced with the plural pronoun *them*.

220. e. Because there are no grammatical errors in this sentence, choice **e** is the best answer.

221. c. The word *there* should be replaced by the possessive pronoun *their*.

222. c. The pronoun *me* should be replaced by the pronoun *I*. In this sentence, *my brother, my Aunt Clarissa*, and *I* is the subject, and the nominative (subject) case is required. *Me* should be only used as an object pronoun.

223. e. Because there are no grammatical errors in this sentence, choice **e** is the best answer.

224. a. This sentence has an agreement problem. The plural pronoun *them* does not agree with the singular noun *glossary*. Therefore, *them* should be replaced by the singular pronoun *it*.

225. b. *Your* should be replaced by *you're*. Because these two words are pronounced alike, they are often confused. *Your* indicates possession and *you're* is the contraction of *you are*.

226. e. Because there are no grammatical, idiomatic, logical, or structural errors in this sentence, **e** is the best answer.

227. e. Because there are no grammatical, idiomatic, logical, or structural errors in this sentence, **e** is the best answer.

SET 20 (Page 46)

228. b. The correct form of the pronoun is *me* (objective case).

229. c. The correct pronoun is *who*, because it refers to a person, and it is the subject form of *who* (not the object form, *whom*), because *who* is doing something, making candied figs.

230. b. The pronoun agrees in number with the noun to which it refers.

231. b. The antecedent, *George and Michael*, is plural, so the plural pronoun *their* is the correct choice.

232. c. The pronoun that agrees in number with the noun to which it refers, *artichoke*.

233. c. The pronoun *them* agrees with the plural noun *flowers*.

234. d. *She and I* is the subject of the sentence, so the subjective case is needed.

235. a. The possessive case is used before the word *taking*, because it functions like a noun in this sentence.

SET 21 (Page 46)

236. b. There are two potential problems in this sentence: 1) the grammatical agreement between the nouns *Kendra or Zoë* and the pronoun *her*; and 2) the formation of the verb *to bring*. In choice **b** both of these are correct. Because the sentence reads *Kendra or Zoë*, the pronoun must be singular; only one of them brought the volleyball. *Brought* is the past tense of *bring*. Choice **a** is wrong because the pronoun *their* is plural. Choice **c** is wrong because *there* is not a correct pronoun. Choices **d** and **e** are incorrect because *brang* is not the past tense of *bring*.

237. a. This choice is the only one that uses the proper form of possessive pronouns.

238. c. This choice is best because it is the only one in which there is no shift in person; i.e., If you are looking . . . , you should compare. . . . All of the other choices shift from third person (someone, one, a person) to second person (you).

239. e. This is the only choice to have agreement between the subject and verb and between the pronoun and its antecedent.

240. d. When the relationship between a pronoun and its antecedent is unclear, as it is in this sentence, it should be changed to avoid ambiguity. There are two boys, Andre and Robert, and choice **d** makes the relationship clear: Robert's family moved, and not Andre's family.

SET 22 (Page 47)

241. c. The word *I* should be replaced with the word *me*, because the pronoun is the object, not the subject.

242. d. There are no errors.

243. d. There are no errors.

244. c. The correct pronoun is *I*, not *me*.

245. b. The contraction *who's* is incorrect. The correct usage is the possessive *whose*.

246. b. This sentence contains a shift in number. *Bears* is a plural noun, so the clause should read: *they were growling.*

247. d. There are no errors.

248. c. The contraction *Three's*, which means *Three is*, is the correct usage.

249. a. The correct usage is the possessive *theirs*, not *there's*.

250. a. *Either* is incorrect. Use *either* with *or* and *neither* with *nor*.

251. a. The pronoun *him* is incorrect. *He* should be used because *you* and *he* are the subjects of the dependent clause.

252. b. The contraction *You're* should be replaced with the possessive *Your*.

253. c. This sentence makes a shift in person. It should read: *The committee members should work as hard as they can.*

254. d. There are no errors.

255. d. There are no errors.

SET 23 (Page 49)

256. b. In the other choices, the pronoun reference is ambiguous; it is unclear who is in the hospital.

257. d. The other answers contain unnecessary shifts in person from *I* to *one*, *you*, and *a person*.

258. b. This is the only choice that is clear and unambiguous. All the other choices contain misplaced modifiers, resulting in unclear and illogical statements.

259. c. This is the only choice that is grammatically correct. Choices **a** and **d** use the verbs incorrectly. Choice **b** uses *a* instead of *an* before anthology.

Section 4: Modifiers

SET 24 (Page 53)

260. b. In this sentence *loud* modifies the verb *screamed*. The adverb *loudly* should be used instead of *loud*.

261. e. Because there are no errors in this sentence, choice **e** is the best answer.

262. d. This sentence makes a comparison between Frieda and two other girls (three people); therefore, the superlative *tallest* should be used. *Taller*, the comparative form, is incorrect because it compares only two people.

263. e. Because there are no errors in this sentence, choice **e** is the best answer.

264. e. Because there are no errors in this sentence, choice **e** is the best answer.

265. d. The double comparative *more cozier* is redundant; just the comparative word *cozier* is sufficient to convey the idea that New York movie theaters will become more comfortable with the addition of love seats.

266. e. Because there are no errors in this sentence, **e** is the best answer.

267. a. In this sentence *close* attempts to modify the verb *resemble*. The adverb *closely* should be used instead of close.

268. d. This sentence makes a comparison between many house guests. Therefore, the superlative word *most* should be used. *More* only compares two things.

269. c. In this sentence *hesitant* attempts to modify the verb *walked*. The adverb *hesitantly* should be used instead of *hesitant*.

270. a. Use *bad* when modifying a noun; use *badly* when modifying a verb. The verb *treated* should be modified by the adverb *badly*, not the adjective *bad*.

SET 25 (Page 54)

271. a. The missing phrase modifies the verb *are armed* and creates a comparison between two types of people, heroes and villains. Therefore you need a comparative form of the adverb *heavily*.

272. c. The comparison is between two things, a cake made last week and a cake made this week; choices **a** and **d** can be ruled out. Choice **b**, *more better*, is redundant. Choice **c**, *better*, is the best choice to make the comparison.

273. d. The missing phrase modifies the verb; therefore the sentence requires an adverb. Choices **a** and **b** are adjectives and can be ruled out. Choice **c** makes an unnecessary comparison.

274. b. The comparison is being made among three brothers; therefore this sentence requires a superlative. Choices **a** and **c** only compare two things, and choice **d** is redundant.

275. a. The missing phrases modifies a noun and makes a comparison between two things, what he thought and what it was; therefore the sentence requires a comparative adjective. Choice **b** is an adverb. Choice **c**

does not make a comparison, and choice **d** is a superlative, a comparison of three or more things. Choice **a**, *more terrifying,* is the best choice.

276. d. Use *fewer* with nouns that can be counted.

SET 26 (Page 55)

277. d. Adjectives modify nouns and adverbs modify verbs. In choice **d**, the adjectives *frightening* and *unhappy* correctly modify the noun *ending*. In choices **a** and **b**, the adverb *frighteningly* incorrectly attempts to modify a noun. In choice **c**, the adverb— *unhappily*—incorrectly attempts to modify a noun. Choice **e** is unnecessarily wordy.

278. b. The sentence makes a comparison between Mandela and all other spokespersons; therefore, the superlative form *most* should be used. Choices **a** and **d** are wrong because they use the comparative *more.* Choice **c** is wrong because the word *prominently* is an adverb and cannot modify the noun *spokesperson.* Choice **e** is wrong because it uses the word *like* incorrectly.

279. a. The word *than* is a conjunction used to indicate a comparison, and used as a conjunction, it is followed by the the pronoun *I.* The word *conservatively* is an adverb modifying the verb *dresses.* Choice **a** is the only one that correctly makes the comparison and uses the adverb correctly.

280. e. This is the correct choice because the sentence does not contain a double negative. The other choices either use two negative words within a single sentence or use an incorrect comparative form of easy.

281. a. The sentence compares an individual and an entire crowd of individuals; therefore it

requires a superlative. Only choice **a** coherently uses the superlative *happiest* to make the comparison among all the many people in the crowd.

282. d. When a comparison is made, the word *fewer* is used with nouns that can be counted; the word *less* is used with quantities that cannot be counted.

283. d. This sentence makes a comparison between strip mining and all other types of mining; therefore, it requires a superlative. Choices **a** and **b** compare only two things while choice **e** inappropriately uses an adverb. Choice **c** uses a double superlative and is redundant.

SET 27 (Page 56)

284. d. There are no errors.

285. a. The adjective *sad* should be replaced with the adverb *sadly,* which correctly modifies the verb *wandered.*

286. a. This sentence contains a double negative.

287. d. There are no errors.

288. d. There are no errors.

289. a. This sentence has a usage error: *fewer* cookies, not *less* cookies.

290. d. There are no errors.

291. a. *Between* is only used to refer to two things. *Among* is the correct word to use in this sentence.

292. d. There are no errors.

293. c. *Most awfulest* is a double superlative, and therefore redundant.

SECTION 5: PARAGRAPH DEVELOPMENT

SET 28 (Page 58)

294. a. This is the best choice because it is the only one that refers to recycling containers, which is the main focus of this paragraph. The other choices are statements about recycling in general.

295. b. This is the only choice that mentions telecommuting, which is the main focus of this paragraph. The other choices are too general.

296. c. This choice refers to "unreasonable searches," which is the main focus of this paragraph. Choice **a** can be ruled out because this idea is not developed by the other two sentences. Choices **b** and **d** do not relate to the topic of unreasonable searches.

297. b. This choice clearly fits with the main focus of the paragraph, which is the skill that is needed to hand-rear orphaned baby birds. Choice **a** is too vague to be a topic sentence. Choices **c** and **d** introduce other topics.

298. c. The main focus of the paragraph is the height of a wave. This is the only choice that introduces that topic.

299. a. The paragraph expresses the writer's opinion about respect for the law. Choices **b** and **d** can be ruled out because they are irrelevant to the main topic. Choice **c** can also be eliminated because it discusses respect for other people, not respect for the law.

300. b. Choice **b** addresses both of Gary's vanities: his person and his situation. Choice **a** deals only with Gary's vanity of person. Choice **c**

deals only with his vanity of position. Choice **d** is not supported in the passage.

301. d. *Changing the course of history* and *nations going to war* implies that the subject of the paragraph is history; these phrases also connote danger and intrigue.

302. a. This is the only choice that is in keeping with the main focus of the paragraph. Although dogs are mentioned in the paragraph, choices **b** and **c** can be ruled out because Sentences 2 and 3 do not logically follow either choice.

303. b. This choice focuses the paragraph by speaking of a particular patterned corridor, as is described in the rest of the paragraph. Choices **a** and **c** only speak of patterned corridors in general. Choice **d** is contradicted in the passage.

304. b. This choice is most relevant to the rest of the paragraph, which is about protecting children from swallowing dangerous medications. Choices **a** and **d** do not mention danger; choice **c** does not mention protection and is also written in a different style than the rest of the paragraph.

305. a. This sentence contrasts writers who endanger their lives in order to have something to write about with those who do not. The rest of the paragraph illustrates this statement. Choice **b** is too broad. Choices **c** and **d** contain elements not expressed in the passage.

306. d. This choice specifically defines the kind of hearsay evidence that is admissible in a trial and would be logically followed by a definition of the kind of hearsay evidence that is inadmissible. It works better as a topic sentence than choice **c**, which is more general. Choices **a** and **b** contradict the rest of the paragraph.

307. c. Choice **c** is the only choice that prepares the reader for the fact that the paragraph constitutes a set of instructions for workers.

308. d. Choice **d** is the only sentence that focuses on both the tickler and its usefulness to secretaries, and therefore is relevant to all the other sentences in the paragraph. Choices **a** and **b** are too general to effectively focus the paragraph; choice **c** is too narrow.

309. c. This choice focuses most sharply on the main topic of the paragraph—muscle atrophy and bone loss. Choices **a** and **b** are too broad to guide the reader to the focus of the paragraph. Choice **d** is too limited.

310. a. The word *rather* indicates a contrast to whatever came before. Choice **a** is the only sentence that guides the reader to the contrast between the old definition of asthma and the new. Choices **b** and **c** are less precisely related to the new understanding of asthma. Choice **d** is not related at all.

311. a. Choice **a** is more specific than the other choices and more sharply focused toward the entire paragraph. Choices **b** and **d** are more vague and general, and choice **c** is written in a slightly different, more upbeat style.

SET 29 (Page 64)

312. a. Choice **a** expands on the topic sentence. Choices **b** and **c** do not relate directly to indoor pollution. The style of choice **d** is more informal than that of the topic sentence.

313. c. This choice directly illustrates the topic sentence. Choice **a** does not mention the Middle Ages, choice **b** does not mention red hair, and choice **d** is unrelated to the topic sentence.

314. a. Choice **a** relates directly to self-medication. The other choices do not.

315. c. The idea expressed in the topic sentence is counterintuitive, as stated in choice **c**. (The words *This idea* also gives an important clue, since an idea is the subject of the topic sentence.) The other choices do not relate directly to the nature of light.

316. b. Choice **b** elaborates on the topic sentence. Choices **a** and **c** are not related to it. Choice **d** is wrong because being promoted to a more responsible position isn't something we think of as having to face.

317. c. Choice **c** expands on the list of good reasons for working for the INS. The other choices are simply neutral facts.

318. d. Choice **d** helps explode the myth spoken of in the topic sentence by giving alternatives to student loans. The other choices do not deal directly with the idea expressed in the topic sentence.

319. b. The topic sentence is obviously from a contract and speaks of an agreement. Choice **b** goes on to explain, in the language of a contract, what that agreement is and so is more closely related to the topic sentence than the other choices.

320. d. This is the only choice that logically follows the topic: It gives reasons why the public is fascinated with Marilyn Monroe. The other choices do not follow the topic sentence.

321. d. Only this choice deals with learning how to accept oneself and then relate it to another person. Choices **a** and **c** are both irrelevant to the topic sentence. Choice **b** states the exact opposite of the topic sentence.

322. a. This is clearly the only choice that logically follows the statement about juries in colonial times. Choices **b** and **c** can be ruled out because they do not refer back to colonial times. Choice **d** refers to colonial times but not to juries.

323. c. This choice develops the topic sentence by following up on information about replacing the QWERTY keyboard with another system. Choices **a** and **b** veer away from the topic. Choice **d** seems to contradict the topic sentence.

324. b. This is the only choice that develops the topic sentence. Choice **a** does not even mention gingko. Choice **c** is redundant because Europe is part of the world. Choice **d**, by referring to an old study, veers completely away from the topic.

325. a. This is the best choice because it directly follows the information that the earth is ancient and complex. Choice **b** changes the topic to mammals. Choice **c** also strays from the topic sentence. Choice **d** changes the topic to Darwin.

SET 30 (Page 67)

326. d. The passage is about the cassowary bird, not about human beings. Sentence 4 is irrelevant to the topic.

327. c. The passage is about the nature of storytelling and has nothing to do with writing programs.

328. b. The passage has to do with the confusion involved in getting online. The price of computers is irrelevant to the main topic.

329. c. The focus of the paragraph is ratatouille, not zucchini.

330. c. This is the only sentence that does not mention sleepwalking, which is the subject of the passage.

331. d. Although there is a connection between Lyme disease and deer ticks, this connection is not made in the paragraph.

332. d. The tone of this sentence is upbeat and perky, whereas the other sentences are quietly professional.

333. b. This is the only sentence that mentions religion or any human activity at all. The other sentences define the solstices in lay science terms.

334. a. There is no mention of TV in the other sentences. Also this sentence has a more casual tone than the others.

335. b. This choice has the objective tone of a textbook and is a general statement. The other choices describe a particular child and are written in a fictional style.

336. b. Choices **a, c,** and **d** list specific characteristics of the two different types of ghosts, benevolent (good) and malevolent (bad). Choice **b** is just an ironic observation on the general subject of ghosts.

337. d. Choices **a, b,** and **c** deal with the characteristics of sociopaths. Choice **d** simply talks about criminals, most of whom are distinguished from sociopaths in the very first sentence.

338. b. This choice has Eleanor Roosevelt as its focus. The other choices focus on Jessie Street.

339. a. Choice **a** addresses the benefits of being able to exercise even if the weather is bad. The remainder of the paragraph focuses on the benefits of exercising without fancy equipment or health clubs.

340. c. The paragraph as a whole deals, not with how to improve motivation of team members (choice **c**), but with making the most of their talents.

341. c. This choice is a general statement about CO poisoning. The other choices all relate to a firefighter's specific duties in dealing with victims of CO poisoning.

SET 31 (Page 71)

342. d. This is the correct chronological order of the events described in the paragraph.

343. c. Sentence 2 gives an overview of what the paragraph is about. Sentence 3 gives specific reasons why Sentence 2 is correct. Sentence 1 gives the reason why Sentence 3 is correct.

344. b. Sentence 1 provides a general prison rule. Sentence 4, with the word *however*, notes an exception to the general rule. Sentence 2, with the word *usually*, gives an example of the exception. Sentence 3 tells how the example is applied in practice.

345. b. Sentence 3 is the topic sentence, and states the purpose of the Peace Corps. Sentence 2 describes the kind of people who join the Peace Corps. Sentence 1 gives a stipulation for the people who join.

346. a. In this choice, the order is chronological. In Sentence 4, they take Grandma to the Greyhound station. In Sentence 2, the bus has not yet moved away from the station. In Sentence 1 the bus jolts away but is still in town. In Sentence 3 the bus (at least in the narrator's mind) is out on the open highway.

347. a. Sentence 1 is the topic sentence. Sentence 4 defines the term double jeopardy used in Sentence 1; Sentence 2 gives another definition, signaled by also; sentence 3 begins with the word *Finally* and gives the last definition.

348. c. Sentence 3 is the general topic sentence. Sentence 2 repeats the word *images* to make a link to the topic sentence. Sentence 3 gives the details of the example; Sentence 1 provides another more general example and offers an explanation for the idea presented in the topic sentence.

349. a. Sentence 2 sets the stage—this is a memory. After that, the order is chronological: In Sentence 1 the man tries to teach his son how to pitch. In Sentence 4 he wasn't interested, so he gave up. Sentence 3 logically follows—the memory of giving up makes him feel sad and guilty.

350. d. Sentence 4 sets the reader up to expect a discussion of a procedure, the writing of reports of a fire. Sentence 3 tells how you can find the right report forms. Sentence 1 leads logically into Sentence 2.

351. a. Sentence 2 is the topic sentence. Sentence 1 provides reasons for the procedure described in the topic sentence. Sentence 3 gives further definition as a conclusion.

352. d. The word *Yet* at the beginning of Sentence 1 is a clue that this is not the beginning sentence. Sentences 4 and 1 are the only ones that logically follow each other, so the other choices can be ruled out.

353. c. Sentence 1 is the topic sentence and states the general situation. Sentence 2 poses a question about the situation in the topic sentence. Sentence 4 offers the response. Sentence 3 concludes the paragraph as it gives a reminder about the original goal.

354. b. Sentence 2 is the topic sentence, introducing the subject. Sentence 3 expands the topic, and Sentence 1 gives more definition to the Native American art form.

355. a. This is the only logical order for the paragraph. Sentence 1 introduces the topic; sentences 2 and 3 develop the topic.

SET 32 (Page 74)

356. b. Paragraph 2 contradicts the misconceptions potential adopters of racing greyhounds might have about the breed. Choice **b** states that certain popular beliefs about greyhounds are erroneous and acts as a transition to the facts that follow in the paragraph. Choice **a** does not focus on contradicting the misinformation; also, the phrase, even so, appears to agree with the misconceptions rather than contradict them. Choice **c** does not focus on the argument; instead, it repeats information given in the previous sentence. Choice **d**, rather than supporting the main purpose of the paragraph—which is to dispel myths about racing greyhounds—actually contradicts information in Parts 6 and 7.

357. b. The possessive pronoun *their* is correct.

358. c. This choice is the best because it retains the writer's informal, reassuring tone and because the information in it furthers the purpose of this paragraph—i.e., the suitability of greyhounds as household pets. This response also is clearly directed at a general audience of householders. Choice **a** is incorrect because the information does not keep with the topic of the paragraph; also, the tone set by the inclusion of a precise statistic is too formal. Choice **b** retains the informal tone of the selection but it provides information already given in the first paragraph and not suitable to the purpose of this paragraph. The tone in choice **d** is argumentative, which defeats the author's purpose of trying to reassure the reader.

359. b. This question tests the ability to recognize a sentence fragment. Although choice **b** does include a subject and a verb, it is a dependent clause because it begins with the adverb *when*. Choices **a**, **c**, and **d** are all standard sentences.

360. a. This question assesses the ability to recognize redundancy in a sentence. Choice **a** removes the redundancy of Part 3 by taking out the word *also*, which repeats the meaning of the introductory phrase *in addition to*. Choice **b** is incorrect because the passage only mentions one patrol, so making the word plural would not make sense. Choice **c** suggests an unnecessary correction in verb tense. Choice **d** suggests a change that would suggest that the writer is talking about all fires, rather than specifically about the arson fires that are the subject of the passage.

361. c. Choice **c** gives a fact (the percentage of decrease in arson because of the efforts of the Patrol in the past) that supports the statement in the preceding sentence (Part 2) that the Patrol has been effective in reducing arson in the past; this choice also develops the ideas in the paragraph by giving a direct justification of why an increase in the Patrol would help the city achieve its aim of reducing arson. Choice **a** does add information that is on topic, but it fails to connect that activity with its result. Choice **b** adds a factual detail about the size of the increase in the patrol, but it does not develop the idea in Part 2—why the patrol has been important in fighting arson. Choice **d** strays from the topic of the paragraph, and the passage as a whole, arson reduction; instead it adds information about unemployment and the mayor's popularity.

362. d. This question tests the ability to recognize standard sentence structure. Part 2 is an incorrectly punctuated compound sentence, a comma splice. Choice **d** correctly joins the two simple sentences into a compound one by using a semicolon in place of the comma. Choice **a** creates an error in subject-verb agreement. Choice **b** is incorrect because a dash cannot join two simple sentences into a compound one. Choice **c** turns the first phrase of the sentence, *Deciding on the hamburger steak special,* into a dangling modifier.

363. b. This question assesses the ability to recognize the correct use of modifiers. The phrase *After tasting each of the dishes on my plate* is a dangling modifier; the sentence does not have a subject pronoun this phrase could modify. Choice **b** is correct because it supplies the missing subject pronoun *I.* Choices **a, c,** and **d** are incorrect because they let the modification error stand; none of them provide a subject pronoun the phrase could modify.

SET 33 (Page 78)

364. b. This question assesses the ability to recognize the correct agreement of subject and verb. Choice **b** is correct because it uses the third person plural of the verb to be, *are,* which agrees in number and person with the subject *fats, oils, and sweets.* Choice **a** is wrong because it does not correct the subject-verb agreement problem; instead it removes an optional comma between *fats* and *and.* Choice **c** is incorrect because it does not correct the agreement error, instead making an unnecessary change in vocabulary from *should* to *must.* Choice **d** is incorrect because it does not correct the agreement problem; instead it creates an error by misplacing the modifier *only* between *sweets* and *these.*

365. d. This question tests the ability to recognize the logical connection of ideas in a paragraph and to recognize grammatical consistency. Choice **d** gives a generalization (the usefulness of the food guide for busy people who are trying to improve nutrition), followed by an example in the next sentence (the ease of shopping while following the guide). Choice **a** is incorrect because, although it provides the generalization for the subsequent example, it contains an error in pronoun/antecedent agreement (using the pronoun *you,* which disagrees in person with the antecedent, *people*). Choice **b** is incorrect because it adds information (about the guide as a visual aid) irrelevant to the development and order of ideas in the passage. Choice **c** is incorrect because it contains the same pronoun/antecedent agreement problem as choice **a**, and the sentence does not respect the order of ideas in the paragraph; it returns, in the second paragraph of the passage, to information and ideas that are more appropriate to the first paragraph.

366. a. Choice **a** is correct because a comma after the word *pyramid* in Part 5 closes off the parenthetical phrase between the subject, *servings*, and the predicate, *should*. Choice **b** is incorrect because it introduces an incomplete comparison into Part 1. Choice **c** is incorrect because, by removing the preposition *of*, it introduces a faulty subordination in Part 7. Choice **d** is incorrect because a colon after *is* would separate the verb from its object.

367. b. The word *appraised,* meaning judged, does not make sense in the context; the correct word for the context is *apprised,* meaning informed. Choices **a, c,** and **d** are all incorrect because the words incriminate, criteria, and ascertain are all used correctly in context.

368. c. The information in Part 5 continues the description of what judges must ascertain about such cases, which began in Part 3. Skipping next to the responsibilities of officers and back to judges, as happens in the passage as it stands, is confusing.

Choices **a** and **b** are incorrect because they introduce examples before the passage states what the examples are supposed to show. Choice **d** is incorrect because deleting Part 2 removes the statement from which all the paragraph's examples and information follow.

369. a. Part 1 contains a run-on sentence; the conjunction *however* requires the use of either a colon or a semicolon before it in order to link two sentences. The other choices are incorrect because the parts they indicate contain standard sentences.

370. c. This choice supplies the third person singular verb, *shows*, which agrees in number and person with the subject, *One completed NASA study*. The second study mentioned in the sentence may be mistaken for a part of the subject, which would make it compound and plural; however, the second study is enclosed by commas, thus making it a parenthetical expression and not a part of the subject. Choice **a** is incorrect because it introduces an error in pronoun/antecedent agreement between *problems* and *it*. Choice **b** is incorrect because it removes a hyphen necessary to the creation of compound adjectives. Choice **d** is incorrect because it creates an error in pronoun/antecedent agreement between *scientists* and *they*.

371. b. The topic of the paragraph is about the ecology of an area; it does not specifically address environmental organizations.

372. c. Since the term *environmental groups* is not a proper noun, it does not need to be capitalized. Choices **a, b,** and **d** are gramatically incorrect.

373. b. Part 5 contains the comparative form *more*, but the sentence only includes one side of the comparison. The phrase *someone . . . may feel more tired* is an incomplete comparison because it does not state what people feel more tired than. Choices **a, c,** and **d** are incorrect because these parts do not contain incomplete or faulty comparisons.

374. a. This question requires the ability to infer the logical relationships between ideas in a sequence. In this case, relationships are, first, between stated fact and the conclusion or hypothesis drawn from the fact (*Since*); and, second, between the hypothesis and a particular illustration supporting the hypothesis (*For example*).

SET 34 (Page 82)

375. d. This question calls on the ability to identify standard usage of the possessive. Choice **d** is correct because the word *researchers* is actually a possessive noun, and so an apostrophe must be added. Choices **a** and **c** are incorrect because they substitute misused homonyms for the words given. Choice **b** is incorrect because it contains a faulty pronoun/antecedent—the *microprobes* have a diminutive width, not the brain.

376. b. In Part 4, the adverb *typically* is misused as an adjective to modify the noun wire. The other choices do not contain nonstandard uses of modifiers.

377. c. The phrases *since they [microprobes] are slightly thinner than a human hair* and *because of their [microprobes'] diminutive width* contain the same information.

378. b. The predicate does not match the subject grammatically, which is necessary when using the verb *is:* A passenger-created disturbance doesn't match by playing . . . or creating.

379. c. This choice makes use of parallel structure because the list of the conductors' obligations are all expressed in the same subject/verb grammatical form: *Conductors will wait, will allow, will not allow.* In choices **a, b,** and **d,** the parallelism of the list is thrown off by the last item in the list, which changes the subject of its verb from operators to passengers.

380. b. Part 6 contains a nonstandard use of a preposition. The standard idiom is *comply with* rather than *comply to.* Choices **a, c,** and **d** do not contain nonstandard uses of prepositions.

381. a. Part 3 contains a sentence fragment; the sentence is a dependent clause. Choices **b, c,** and **d** are incorrect because they indicate standard sentences.

382. c. The main purpose of this paragraph is strictly informational, to outline the President's proposals for improving education in the U.S., and choice **c** focuses the reader's attention on the list of proposals. Choice **a** contains information that contradicts the material in the passage, for it states a limitation of the proposals. Choice **b** essentially gives information about what specific effect the proposals might have, which is out of place in a paragraph that is only aimed at listing the proposals. Choice **d** makes an argumentative claim about the necessity for certain of the proposals, which is again out of place in a paragraph that seeks only to list the proposals.

383. b. The subject pronoun *they* is used erroneously in Part 2 as a direct object of the verb. The reflexive pronoun *themselves*, which may be used as a direct object, is a better choice.

384. d. In Part 3, the relative pronoun *that* is necessary to properly subordinate the clause *programs that meet this rising demand* to the main clause. Retaining the word *than* would introduce a faulty comparison into the sentence. Choice **a** is incorrect because the comma it seeks to remove is necessary to indicate the restrictive nature of the adjective *more*. Choice **b** is incorrect because inserting a comma after *statistics* produces a comma fault error. Choice **c** is incorrect because it erroneously inserts the adverb *there* in a context where the possessive pronoun *their* is required.

385. b. Part 6 contains a run-on sentence. Choices **a, c,** and **d** are incorrect because they all contain standard sentences.

386. a. The semicolon in Part 1 must be followed by an independent clause, and here it is followed by a dependent clause. Choices **b, c,** and **d** are incorrect because they all contain standard sentences.

387. b. The underlined word in Part 2 needs to be made into a possessive noun. Choice **c** is incorrect because it uses a plural possessive where a singular possessive is required. Choices **a** and **d** are incorrect because they insert an adjective where a possessive noun is needed.

SET 35 (Page 86)

388. c. End quotation marks must be inserted before the tag phrase, *Riley said*. Choice **a** is incorrect because the quotation marks are necessary to begin the quotation again after the tag phrase. Choice **b** is incorrect because it creates a comma fault. Choice **d** is incorrect because it introduces an unidiomatic usage of a preposition.

389. d. The expression *a lot* should be replaced because it is imprecise and because its conversational tone does not match the precise diction of the paragraph. Choices **a, b,** and **c** are word choices that have exact meanings and match the formal tone of the paragraph.

390. d. Part 2 acts as a topic sentence for the paragraph of quotation that follows it. In other words, combining the second and third paragraph is in order because they are on the same topic, and combining them makes the subject of the third paragraph clearer to a reader. Choice **a** would actually muddy the meaning of the last three sentences, since it would reverse the order of Parts 6 and 7, when Part 7 logically follows from Part 6. Choice **b** is incorrect because it would edit out information that is important to the understanding of Part 7. Choice **c** is incorrect because it does not make sense to combine these two sentences as they are on different topics.

391. c. The first paragraph mentions that saving room for herbs such as lavender, sage, thyme, and parsley is a characteristic of a thrifty gardener, but fails to explain why it is a sign of thrift. Choice **a** is incorrect because it removes information that is vital to explaining why the plants mentioned in Part 1 are appropriate to a gardener who has little time. Choice **b** is incorrect because reversing the order of the sentences moves the demonstrative pronoun *these* in Part 2 too far away from its antecedent. Choice **d** is incorrect because the passage does not indicate that growing roses is easy in general; rather, it suggests particular types of roses (hardy species) as appropriate to a garden that requires little time for maintenance.

392. a. This sentence creates a transition between the idea of harvesting food from a garden and the proper way of planting in order to achieve a good yield of food. Choice **b** is incorrect because it is redundant, repeating information already stated in Part 5. Choice **c** contains information that is on the subject matter of the first paragraph does not matter and is, thus, off-topic in the second. Choice **d** is off-topic and does not match the main idea of the paragraph; it mentions time-consuming work in a paragraph on the subject of gardening that takes a moderate amount of time.

393. b. The word *lavished* should be substituted for languished because it makes no sense in the context.

394. c. Part 4 contains a nonstandard verb form, brung, as the past-tense form of *to bring*; the correct verb *is brought*. Choices **a**, **b**, and **d** are incorrect because they do not contain nonstandard usages of verbs.

395. b. Part 3 contains a sentence fragment, for there is no main verb in the sentence. Choices **a**, **c**, and **d** are incorrect because they are complete sentences.

SET 36 (Page 88)

396. b. Part 3 requires a comma before the coordinate conjunction *so*. Choice **d** is incorrect because it already shows a comma separating the two independent clauses. Choices **a** and **c** are incorrect because each contains only one independent clause.

397. a. This answer is in the simple past tense, which is the tense used throughout the paragraph. Choices **b**, **c**, and **d** are incorrect because they suggest tenses inconsistent with the tense of the rest of the paragraph.

398. b. The context requires that the noun *renown* be replaced by the adjective *renowned*. Choice **a** is incorrect because the change to *when* makes no sense in the context; it would imply that Augustus grew up before immigrating. Choice **c** incorrectly inserts the contraction of subject and verb *it is* in a context where the possessive pronoun *its* is required. Choice **d** is incorrect because it introduces a diction error into the sentence.

399. b. The semicolon in Part 2 is used incorrectly to introduce a list. In choices **a**, **c**, and **d**, the semicolon correctly separates two independent clauses.

400. c. The expressions *year-round* and *in all seasons* repeat the same idea. Choices **a**, **b**, and **d** are incorrect because none of these sentences contain unnecessary repetition. Part 4 may seem to, at first; however, the words *hot* and *humid* are described in the rest of the sentence to be more interesting and specific.

401. b. The subject of Part 3 is climate and therefore requires the third-person singular form of the verb to be—*is*. Choice **c** is incorrect because the comma is correctly placed after an introductory phrase. Choice **a** incorrectly inserts the possessive pronoun *its* in a context where the contraction of subject and verb *it is* is required. Choice **d** is incorrect because the comma is necessary to close off the interruptive phrase, *whether in the back country or at established campgrounds*, between the subject and verb.

402. c. Part 3 provides information about the Surgeon General's findings that are off the topic of the announcement about the FDA's ruling about the labeling of milk. Choices **a**, **b**, and **d** are incorrect because all of these sentences add information about the FDA ruling, its reasons, and its effects.

403. a. The word *imply*, meaning to express or indicate indirectly, is misused in the context of Part 4; the word *infer*, to surmise, makes sense in the context. In choice **b** the change from noun to adverb is incorrect, for there is no verb for the adverb *crucially* to modify properly. Choice **c** is incorrect because the phrase *set of* implies the plural criteria rather than the singular criterion. Choice **d** is incorrect because it introduces an error in standard English diction.

404. a. In Part 1, the adjective *good* is misused as an adverb; it needs to be replaced by the adverb *well*.

405. a. In Part 4, the verb *assure*, to make certain, is nonsensical in the context; it should be replaced by the verb *assume*, to suppose or take for granted. Choices **b**, **c**, and **d** are incorrect because all these words are used properly in their context.

406. d. The paragraph consistently uses the pronoun *you;* therefore, the inconsistent use of *our* should be replaced by *your*. Choice **a** is incorrect because the comma is necessary before the coordinate conjunction *but*. Choice **b** is incorrect because insertion of a colon would incorrectly divide a phrase. Choice **c** is incorrect because it would introduce an error of tense shift into the paragraph.

SET 37 (Page 91)

407. a. The word *greek* in Part 2 should be capitalized. Nationalities and languages require capitalization. Choice **b** is incorrect because a person's title, given before his or her name, should be capitalized, while **d** is incorrect because the title should not be capitalized when no name is given. Choice **c** is incorrect because the names of seasons are not capitalized.

408. a. Part 1 contains a run-on sentence. It requires a semicolon after the parentheses and before *we*. Choices **b**, **c**, and **d** are incorrect because the numbered parts they indicate all contain standard sentences.

409. b. The context requires a word meaning to surrender or yield, so choice **b** is correct. The other choices are incorrect because each has the wrong meaning for the context of the sentence.

410. d. To make the pair of verbs in the sentence parallel, *overlooking* should be changed to *overlooks* to match the form of the verb *towers*. Choice **a** is incorrect because the change would convert Part 7 into a run-on sentence. Choice **b** is incorrect because *Irish*, as the name of a people, must be capitalized. Choice **c** is incorrect because the word *running* is functioning as an adjective here; the verb *run* would make nonsense of the sentence.

411. d. A comma is required after an introductory dependent clause. Choice **a** would introduce a comma fault, separating a verb from its object. Choice **b** is incorrect because the semicolon would have to be followed by a complete sentence, which is not the case. Choice **c** is incorrect because removing the colon would create a run-on sentence.

412. c. Choices **a** and **b** would cause an unwarranted shift in tense from past (in which most of the passage is written) to present. Choice **d** would change the correctly written noun, *effect*, to an incorrect verb form. (*Affect* is a verb, except when used as a noun to denote a person's emotional expression, or lack thereof, as in: *He has a joyless affect.*)

413. b. The adjective *shallow* in Part 5 actually modifies the verb *set*; therefore, the adjective should be revised to be the adverb *shallowly*. Choices **a, c,** and **d** are incorrect because none of them contain a nonstandard use of a modifier.

414. c. The proper noun *Lake* must be made possessive because it is followed by the gerund *arriving*. Choice **a** is incorrect because it introduces a comma fault into the sentence. Choices **b** and **d** introduce errors in diction into the sentence.

SET 38 (Page 93)

415. c. This paragraph is about how to handle business phone calls. Reversing the order of Parts 9 and 13 would cause the paragraph to follow the natural order of the beginning to the end of a phone conversation. Choice **a** is incorrect because the information in Part 9, though misplaced, is essential information and should not be deleted. Choice **b** is incorrect because both Parts 8 and 13 need to come near the beginning of the paragraph, for they contain information about handling messages. Choice **d** is incorrect because the addition of such a sentence would repeat information already given or implied in the rest of the paragraph.

416. b. This sentence requires the adverb *then* in this context. Choice **a** is incorrect because it would introduce a problem of agreement between the pronoun *they* and its antecedent *pitch*. Choice **c** is incorrect because it would introduce a problem in subject/verb agreement. Choice **d** is incorrect because the possessive rather than the plural of the noun *boss* is necessary in this context.

417. d. The verb *depend* is, idiomatically, followed by the preposition *on*; in Part 10 it is wrongly followed by *in*. Choices **a, b,** and **c** are incorrect because none of them contain nonstandard uses of prepositions.

418. a. The antecedent of the pronoun *they* in this sentence is *someone*. Since *someone* is singular, the corrected subject pronoun should be *he* or *she*.

419. c. The sentence requires the contraction *we're*, short for *we are*. It is all right to use a contraction because the writer uses contractions elsewhere in the passage. Choice **a** is incorrect because it introduces an error in modifiers. Choice **b** is incorrect because a semicolon must be followed, here, by a full sentence. Choice **d** is incorrect because the singular *a deadline* would disrupt the parallelism of the list, the other elements of which are plural.

420. a. Choice **a** is the most logical sentence because it addresses the principles of the topic—Kwaanza. Choices **b**, **c**, and **d** would support choice **a**. They would not work as the topic sentence.

421. d. Part 2 contains a run-on sentence. These two sentences should be separated with a period after *culture*. Choices **a**, **b**, and **c** are incorrect because they all contain standard sentences.

422. a. Another sentence is needed to add the information that the program is only for passengers leaving the bus, not those boarding it. This information is implied in the paragraph but not directly stated; without the direct statement, the paragraph is confusing, and the reader must read between the lines to get the information. Choice **b** is incorrect because it removes an important instruction to drivers, rather than clarifying the paragraph's point. Choice **c** is incorrect because it adds information that contradicts the point the paragraph is making. Choice **d** is incorrect because it would place intervening material between the ideas of what the program is and how it operates; it would disorder the sequence of ideas.

423. a. The subjective pronoun *who* is incorrectly used to refer to the Stop Here Program; the pronoun *which* would be a better choice.

424. b. Part 5 contains two sentences linked only by a comma; a semicolon is required. Choices **a**, **c**, and **d** are incorrect because they all contain standard sentences.

425. d. In Part 4, a semicolon is used incorrectly to introduce a list; it should be replaced by a colon. Choice **a** is incorrect because the possessive pronoun is required in this context. Choice **b** is incorrect because it would introduce a comma fault between the subject *others* and the verb *were*. Choice **c** is incorrect because the comma is needed to separate items in a list.

SET 39 (Page 96)

426. a. This paragraph is written with powerful verbs. *Was looking* is passive and has little impact in the passage. Choices **b**, **c**, and **d** use the active voice.

427. c. Part 3 says *he were sure*. He is singular and takes the verb *was*. Choices **a**, **b**, and **d** are incorrect because all verbs are used correctly.

428. b. *Cortez* is a proper noun and should begin with a capital letter. Choices **a**, **c**, and **d** would make the sentences grammatically incorrect.

429. d. Commas are used to separate city from country. Choices **a**, **b**, and **c** would make the sentences gramatically incorrect.

430. b. Titles of books are always underlined or italicized. Short stories (choice **a**) are punctuated with quotation marks. Author's names (choice **c**) are not italicized. Copyrights do not need italics (choice **d**).

431. a. Choice **a** is written in the tone and style reflected in the passage. Choices **b, c,** and **d** are awkward versions of the same details.

432. d. The verb needs to be singular to agree with the singular subject of the sentence, *Theodore Roosevelt.* Choices **a, b,** and **c** are incorrect because they introduce a shift in tense.

433. a. The subject of this paragraph is the appearance and observation of cuttlefish. Choice **a** is about observing cuttlefish in the wild and the laboratory. Choices **b** and **c** stray from the topic of the paragraph. Choice **d,** while having something to do with the appearance of cuttlefish, is written in jargon that is too technical to match the tone of the rest of the passage.

434. c. The double mention in Part 6 of the human-like eyes of the cuttlefish is unnecessarily repetitious.

435. d. The correct choice is *hover,* because to *hoover* is an archaic slang phrase meaning to vacuum the floor. *For* (meaning to indicate the purpose of the action) is the correct preposition for this sentence, so choice **a** is the incorrect choice. Choice **b** is incorrect because *allow* is the right word (*allot,* meaning to apportion, would not make sense). Choice **c** is incorrect, because it would make the sentence ungrammatical with regard to number.

SET 40 (Page 100)

436. c. The word *carnavale* is a foreign word; therefore, it must be italicized. Choice **a** is incorrect because there is no reason to italicize the word *serfs,* an ordinary noun, in the passage. Choice **b** is incorrect

because the definite article is not needed before the word *Carnival* used as a proper noun. Choice **d** is incorrect because the verb *were* is used correctly here, in the subjunctive mood.

437. a. The objective pronoun *her* is misused in Part 1 as a subject pronoun; it needs to be replaced with the pronoun *she.*

438. a. Quotation marks need to be inserted before the quotation is resumed after the interrupting phrase, *the brochure informed her.* Choice **b** is incorrect because the comma is required to set off the interrupting phrase from the quotation. Choice **c** is incorrect because the close quotation marks are necessary before the interrupting phrase. Choice **d** is incorrect because the quotation is not finished; it goes on for another sentence.

439. b. This statement maintains the formal tone established by the rest of the passage. Choices **a, c,** and **d** are still too informal.

440. d. In Part 1, the pronoun *you* needs to be changed to *we* to agree in number and person to the antecedents used earlier in the passage. Choices **a, b,** and **c** are incorrect because none of these sentences contain a nonstandard use of a pronoun.

441. a. *Consequently* means as a result of. The adverbs listed in choices **b, c,** and **d** do not address this sequence.

442. c. Choice **c** reflects the sentiments in the last sentence of the passage. Choices **a, b,** and **d** do not state such a profound effect.

443. d. Part 1 is a fragment and needs a verb to make it a complete sentence. The sentences in choices **a, b,** and **c** are complete.

444. b. The pronoun *my* needs to be changed to *our* to agree in number and person with the pronoun *we*. Choices **a, c,** and **d** fail to correct the pronoun/antecedent agreement problem.

SET 41 (Page 102)

445. b. The main idea of this paragraph is that, while genius has a recognizable pattern, the patterns are extraordinary. Choice **b** directly states that the patterns have the eerie quality of fate. Choice **a** does not focus ideas, but rather repeats material already stated. Choice **c** focuses attention on the side idea of the popular opinions about genius. Choice **d** contains material that is irrelevant to the main idea and argument of the passage.

446. c. The possessive *Mozart's* is required before the gerund *composing*. Choice **a** is incorrect because *too*, meaning excessively, is required in this context, not the preposition *to*. Choice **b** is incorrect because the possessive form does not make sense in this context. Choice **d** is incorrect because *there*, not the possessive pronoun *their*, is required in this context.

447. a. Part 4 contains an error in pronoun/antecedent agreement; the pronoun *they* must be changed to *it* in order to agree in number and person with its antecedent, *regularity*. Choices **b, c,** and **d** are incorrect because they contain standard uses of pronouns.

448. d. Part 6 is a statement about the effect of the play in theater history in general; however, this statement is placed in the midst of a description of the reception of the opening of the play. The paragraph ends with a statement about the play's effect on theater history, so Part 6 should either be moved to the end of the paragraph or removed. Since there is no choice to move Part 6 to the end of the paragraph, choice **d** is the correct answer. Choice **a** is incorrect because it still leaves Part 6 in a position where its meaning is out of place. Choice **b** is incorrect because removing the phrase has little effect on the paragraph; it merely removes a concrete detail. Choice **c** is incorrect because removing Part 9 excises the conclusion that the previous sentence has promised; it is necessary to the development of the paragraph.

449. c. The names of works that can be published on their own should be italicized, even if only part of the title (in this case Godot) is used to designate the work; therefore choice **b** is incorrect. Choice **a** is incorrect because Mr. Godot names a character, not the play. Choice **d** is incorrect because the titles of newspapers must be italicized.

450. c. The comma in Part 5 separates the subject, *critics and playgoers*, from its verb, *greeted*.

451. b. Inserting a comma in Part 2, after the word *opening*, separates the introductory clase from the rest of the sentence. The sentences in choices **a, c,** and **d** are correct as they are written.

452. d. The two independent clauses in Part 2 need a conjunction in order for the sentence to be gramatically correct. Choices **a, b,** and **c** are incorrect because those sentences are correctly written.

453. **c.** *To correctly divide* is a split infinitive. The infinitive is *to divide*. Choices **a**, **b**, and **d** do not make this kind of error.

454. **a.** The context requires a verb that means *to extend beyond*, not *to come before*. The words in the other choices do not have this meaning.

455. **a.** Part 2 is the only interrogatory sentence in the passage. Since it asks a question, it needs a question mark as punctuation.

SET 42 (Page 105)

456. **d.** Since the sentence states that the *system is designed to give*, then it needs *to ensure* as well. Choices **a**, **b**, and **c** are correct as written.

457. **c.** The pronoun *his* should be replaced with *their* in order to agree with *federal employers*. There are no errors in pronoun agreement in choices **a**, **b**, or **d**.

458. **a.** A semicolon should separate two complete sentences (independent clauses); the second half of Part 6 is not a complete sentence but a restatement of a portion of the first half. This makes a colon appropriate. Choices **b** and **c** would create run-on sentences. Choice **d** would incorrectly separate two independent clauses joined by a conjunction (*and*) with a semicolon.

459. **c.** The pronoun is one of the subjects of the sentence, and so it should be changed from the object form *him* to the subject form *he*. Choice **a** is incorrect because the comma is necessary before the conjunction. Choice **b** is incorrect because the possessive form is not required in this context. Choice **d** is

incorrect because *their*, meaning belonging to *them*, is correct in this context.

460. **a.** Part 5 is the only sentence fragment in this passage. It needs a subject in order to express a complete thought.

461. **d.** The word *recently* is the best contrast to *Finally though* in Part 2. Choices **a**, **b**, and **c** indicate time lapses that would not necessarily take place in the context of the passage.

462. **a.** The comma is needed to set off the introductory clause from the independent clause. Making the changes stated in choices **b**, **c**, or **d** would create a nonstandard sentence.

463. **b.** The phrase *at the ceiling* should be replaced with *on the ceiling*.

464. **c.** The pronoun *it* should be changed to *they* to agree in number and person with its antecedent, *detectors*. Choices **a**, **b**, and **d** are incorrect because they contain standard uses of pronouns.

465. **c.** The paragraphs are related in that they both talk about the physical effects of extreme heat on people and the treatment of these conditions, but the main subject of each paragraph details a different condition resulting from extreme heat. The second paragraph begins by mentioning that heat stroke is much more serious than the condition mentioned in Paragraph 1, heat exhaustion. Choice **c** best aids the transition by ending the first paragraph with an explanation of the most serious effects of heat exhaustion, thereby paving the way for the contrasting description of the far more serious condition, heat stroke. Choice **a** is off topic; choices **b** and **d** are both about heat stroke, so they belong in the second paragraph, not the first.

466. b. The main idea of this paragraph is a description of the symptoms and treatment of heat stroke. The information in Part 7 about the most common victims of heat stroke is least relevant to the topic of the paragraph. The other choices, by contrast, all either discuss symptoms or treatment.

467. a. Part 1 is a sentence fragment; it contains no main verb.

SET 43 (Page 108)

468. a. The phrase *what the occupants been doing* needs an auxiliary verb—for example, it might read *what the occupants had been doing*. Choices **b, c,** and **d** are incorrect because they contain standard verb forms.

469. c. Part 2 contains a comma splice; the comma should be replaced with a semicolon. Choices **a, b,** and **d** are incorrect because they contain standard sentences.

470. c. Part 2 expresses two complete thoughts as one. To correct this sentence, a comma should be added after *Greenland* and the conjunction *but* should precede the independent clause.

471. d. Even though it may look like a question, Part 6 is not an interrogatory sentence. It should not be punctuated with a question mark.

472. c. This choice adds the subject *he* in the second sentence, eliminating the dangling modifier *walking down the street*. Otherwise the sentence reads as if the leaves are walking down the street. All other choices ignore the problem of the dangling

modifier and add grammatical mistakes to the sentences.

473. b. This paragraph's purpose is descriptive; it describes the classroom and the corridor outside it. Choice **b** is correct because the information in the sentence adds to the description of the corridor. Choice **a** is incorrect because it adds information that describes the course Howard is to teach, which is not the subject of this paragraph. Choice **c** is incorrect because it adds information about the two buildings mentioned in the first paragraph; therefore, it rightfully belongs in the first paragraph, not the second. Choice **d** is incorrect because it adds information irrelevant to the paragraph.

474. c. Part 6 is a dependent clause with no independent clause to attach itself to; therefore, it is a sentence fragment.

475. d. The word *wreaked* should be replaced in this context by its homonym reeked. Choices **a, b,** and **c** are all incorrect because the words indicated are all used correctly in their context.

SECTION 6: ESSAY QUESTIONS

ESSAY SCORING CRITERIA
Use the scoring guide below to score each of your essays. Better yet, have someone else read your essay and use the scoring guide to help you see how well you have done. Sample essays for the first six essay topics follow this scoring guide.

A **"6" essay** is a highly effective response to the assignment; a few minor errors are allowed. It has the following additional characteristics:

- Good organization and overall coherence
- Clear explanation and/or illustration of main ideas
- Variety of sentence syntax
- Facility in language usage
- General freedom from mechanical mistakes and errors in word usage and sentence structure

A **"5" essay** shows competence in responding to the assigned topic but may have minor errors.

- Competent organization and general coherence
- Fairly clear explanation and/or illustration of main ideas
- Some variety of sentence syntax
- Facility in language usage
- General freedom from mechanical errors and errors in word usage and sentence structure

A **"4" essay** displays competence in response to the assignment. It has the following additional characteristics:

- Adequate organization and development
- Explanation and illustration of some key ideas
- Adequate language usage
- Some mechanical errors and mistakes in usage or sentence structure, but such errors are not consistent

A **"3" essay** shows some competence but is plainly flawed. Additionally, it has the following characteristics:

- Inadequate organization or incomplete development

- Inadequate explanation or illustration of main ideas
- A pattern of mechanical mistakes or errors in usage and sentence structure

A **"2" essay** shows limited competence and is severely flawed. Additionally, it has the following characteristics:

- Poor organization and general lack of development
- Little or no supporting detail
- Serious mechanical errors and mistakes in usage, sentence structure, and word choice

A **"1" essay** shows fundamental lack of writing skill. Additionally, it has the following characteristics:

- Organization that is practically nonexistent and general incoherence
- Severe and widespread writing errors

A **"0" essay** does not address the topic assigned.

SAMPLE ESSAYS, SET 44 (Page 112)

476.

Sample "6" Essay
Though it may seem to contradict the ideal of democracy upon which our public school system is based, requiring public school students to wear uniforms is a good idea. In fact, uniforms would help schools provide a better education to all students by evening out socio-economic differences and improving discipline among students.

Style is important, especially to children and teenagers who are busy trying to figure out who they are and what they believe in. But in many schools today, kids are so concerned about what they wear that clothing becomes a major distraction—even an obsession. Many students today are too busy to study because they're working after school so they can afford the latest fashions. If students were required to wear uniforms, they would have less pressure to be "best dressed" and more time to devote to their studies.

More importantly, the competition over who has the hottest clothes can be devastating to the self-esteem of students from lower-income families. Because uniforms would require everyone to wear the same outfits, students from poorer families would not have to attend school in hand-me-downs nor would they face the kind of teasing they often get from students who can afford name brands. True, students from wealthier families may wear nicer shoes and accessories, but in general the uniforms will create an an atmosphere of equality for all students.

Contrary to what opponents argue, uniforms will not create uniformity. Just because students are dressed the same does not mean they won't be able to develop as individuals. In fact, because uniforms enable students to stop worrying so much about their appearance, students can focus more on who they are on the inside and on what they're supposed to be learning in the classroom.

Furthermore, uniforms will improve discipline in the schools. Whenever a group of people dresses alike, they automatically have a sense of community, a sense of common purpose. Uniforms mean something. School uniforms will constantly remind students that they are indeed in school—and they're in school to learn. Getting dressed for school itself will be a form of discipline that students will carry into the classroom.

Though many students will complain, requiring public school students to wear uniforms makes sense. Students will learn more—both about themselves and about the world around them.

Sample "4" Essay

I don't think that requiring public school students to wear uniforms is a good idea. The way the student dresses makes a powerful statement about who he or she is, and the school years are an important time for them to explore their identities. Uniforms would undermine that. They would also have little, if any, positive affect on students with disipline problems.

Each student has their own personality, and one way he expresses who he is is through his clothing. Clothes are an important way for young people to show others how they feel about themselves and what is important to them. If public school students are forced to wear uniforms, this important form of self-expression will be taken away.

I remember back when I was in junior high school. My parents had given me complete freedom to buy my back to school wardrobe. They took me to the mall and let me choose everything, from sweaters and shirts to socks and shoes. I'll never forget how independent that made me feel. I could choose clothing that I liked. I did make a few bad choices, but at least those were my choices. Students today, I am sure, would feel the same way.

Besides, America values individuality. What happens to that value in an environment where everybody looks the same?

Though disipline in schools is a serious concern, uniforms are not the answer. Disipline problems usually come from a lack of disipline at home, and that's a problem that uniforms can't begin to address. A student who is rowdy in the classroom isn't going to change their behavior because they are wearing a white shirt and tie. In fact, disipline problems might increase if students are required to wear uniforms. Students often make trouble because they want attention. Well-behaved students who used to get attention from how they dressed might now become trouble-makers so they can continue to get attention.

Uniforms are not the answer to the problems public school students face. In fact, because they'll restrict individuality and may even increase disiplinary problems, they'll only add to the problem.

Sample "3" Essay

I don't think that requiring public school students to wear uniforms is a good idea. Each student has their own identity and express who he is through clothing. The school years are an important in finding one's personality. Uniforms would also have little, if any, positive affect on students with disipline problems.

In junior high school I let my children buy their back-to-school wardrobe, anything they wanted. I let them choose everything. I'll never forget how that made them feel. As they would say, awesome! They could choose clothing that they liked.

We are told to be yourself. But how can a young person be in a country where everybody is the same.

Disipline in schools is of a serious concern, uniforms are not the answer. It is the home life of many students that make bad behavior. If the parents use drugs or dont disipline children at home, thats a problem that the school and uniforms can't do anything about. A student who is causing trouble at school isn't going to change their behavior because they are wearing a white blouse or pleated skirt. In fact, disipline problems might even get worse if students are required to wear uniforms because of not getting enough attention about the way he or she is dressed.

Uniforms are not the answer to the problems public school students face. In fact, because they will keep them from being who they are they will make it worse.

Sample "1" Essay

Public school students should wear uniforms to. Not just private school students. I do not want to teach in a private school; but I like them wearing a uniform every day. The look neat and well-groom no matter if they are low income or high income. Social level doesnt matter.

Wearing uniforms is good because they build a sense of community. Everyone from the same school wear the same clothes. The students know if someone is from there school right away. It makes it easier for students, rich or poor, to make friends with people. They don't have to worry about what to wear in the morning because they always know.

Also they don't have to spend as much money on cloths.

Many students think it is unfair that public school students could wear whatever they wanted. Maybe private school students shouldn't wear uniforms either. Then everyone would be able to dress the way they want to and be individulistic.

Some people say uniforms would make bad students behave better. Because they wouldn't always be talking about who has a better sneakers or better jeans. They might have paid more attention in school like they should of, and then everyone could learn more.

477.

Sample "6" Essay

The best way for teachers to boost their students' science test scores is to make students excited by science with real-life examples. Before ever asking students to memorize facts, the teacher should demonstrate a scientific process or even teach students how to experiment for themselves. This allows them to understand the process with their senses before trying to fix it in their intellect.

The following examples could be used to provide anticipation of a lesson to come. First, when studying insects, the teacher might pass around an ant farm in the classroom and let students observe the little anthropods going about their complex, individual tasks before asking the student to read that ants have a rigid social structure, just as people do. If possible, it would be even better to take them on a field trip to see how ants build hills outdoors.

Another example is to let students have hands-on experience with telescopes. Close observation of far-away objects is magical; the rings of Saturn really exist! The Sea of Tranquility, a crater on the moon's surface looks as close as a building on the next block. This introduction to the galaxy and the universe brings the opportunity for lessons about the earth's rotation and about the geophysical facts of the craters that comprise the moon's laughing face. Lessons like these come alive in a way that does not exist in lecture format.

This approach to teaching science should not begin in high school or college but in grade school or even in kindergarten. Scientific facts are important, of course, but without them we have no real understanding. Curiosity is as vital to learning as the ability to memorize, perhaps more so. Curiosity will keep students learning long after they've passed their final test in school.

Sample "4" Essay

Science is important for many reasons, but especially because today's world is based on technology. If other countries get ahead of us in science the consequences may be dire. So it is extremely important for our students to excell.

The first and best way to teach science is to make the student see the practical application of it. For example, if the teacher is teaching botony, she might explain the medical uses of plants. Or if teaching physics, she might show a diagram of a rocket ship. Field trips are a good idea, as well, perhaps to a factory that makes dolls. The point is to make it practical and interesting to boys and girls alike.

When I was in high school I had a teacher named Mr. Wiley who let us mix things in jars and watch the results. Sometimes they were unexpected! Such as a kind of mushroom we planted that was poisonous and reminded us of the horror movies we all loved in those days. Mr. Wiley made it interesting in a personal way, so that it wasn't just dry facts. And he told us the practical uses, such as this particular kind of mushroom is used in the making of certain insect poison.

In this day and age it is important for all of us to know something about science because it affects all aspects of our lives, but for young people it is vital. Their livelihoods—and even their lives—may depend on that knowledge.

Sample "3" Essay

Science is a necesary skill because it can effect each one of us, such as the making of the hydrogen bomb or finding a cure for AIDS. It is responsable for TV, cars, and a host of other items we take for granted. So we all depend on it and need to learn it.

The best way to teach science is to have a good textbook and also good equiptment in the classroom. If the equiptment is poor there is no way they are going to learn it, which is why the poorer schools are behind the richer ones and also behind other countries. Its the most important factor in the classroom today.

Another way to teach science is through field trips and vidio-tapes. There are many tapes in the library and every school should have a good vidio system. Also a good library is important. And there are many places to take the class that they would find intresting.

When I was in school I thought science was boring. I wish I had learned more about it because I think it would make me a better teacher someday as well as better understand the world of technology. If we don't understand technology we are at it's mercy, and it is something we rely on to get us through our lives. Without science we would have no technilogical advances. If other countries are ahead of us it is our own fault for not putting science as a priority.

Sample "1" Essay

Science is importnt and we should teach it to our students in the right way. A scientist coming in to talk would be one way. Also experimints that the students can do. The reason it is important, is other countrys are ahead of us and we may have a war. Then if there tecnoligy is better they will take us over. So it is dangerous not to have students that know alot about science.

If we teach our children to relay too much on science and technoligy what will happen if it fails. If the computers fail we are in serious trouble. Businesses will suffer and medical research will suffer. So science is important and our students should learn but it isnt everything and they should learn that they should study other things to, like how to make a good living for there family.

If we teach science in the right way our country will be better off as well as our children when they are caught up to the new melinnium

SET 45 (Page 112)

478.

Sample "6" Essay

Television has an important place in society for two reasons. First, it is a common denominator that can be used as a teaching tool for kids. Second, it bridges gaps between cultures. With a simple flick of the switch people can tune in and watch Congressional meetings, travel down the Ganges, or see the Scottish highlands. They can learn about other cultures, cooking, or ar-

chitecture. They can witness events half a world away as soon as they take place.

Since everyone in every classroom from kindergarten to college has been exposed to television, its programs can bring about lively discussions and a meeting of the minds. Television opens windows on the world that are unique. It helps students see more of the world than any generation before them. Given the right focus in a classroom, it can be the start of a writing exercise or a debate. The skills learned in these kinds of exercises prepare students for more complicated tasks later on in life.

By watching engaging, educational television programming, people from all walks of life can learn about others. Knowing and understanding the habits, religion, and cultural traits of people from distant parts of the globe helps bring the world closer together. It makes people more tolerant of others and can only promote peace in a global village that becomes increasingly smaller every day we live. Its place in society is vital.

Sample "4" Essay

Many people say they don't watch television, and I say good for them! There is very little on TV today that is worth watching. And yet, for all that, it has an important place in society. I believe, for example, that it is an excellent teaching tool for kids who have had less than a sterling formal education in the lower grades. It's something they can relate to and something they will have in common with the other people in their class. It's something they have in common with the teacher, for that matter. And that is all-important.

Television opens a window on the world that is unique. It helps students to see more of the world than any generation before them has been able to see. With a simple flick of the switch they can look in and watch the goings-on in congress; or travel down the Ganges river or see the Scotish highlands. They can learn about other cultures, learn how to cook or build a house. They can witness events half a world away as soon as they take place.

Here is one advantage of television, as it can be used as a teaching tool. In classrooms today, especially in community colleges, for example, there are students from every strata of society, from many different social classes. Television is one thing they have in common and can bring about lively discussions and a meeting of the minds. Rich and poor alike, privileged or under privileged, all have looked through that tiny window and see wonders and horrors, current events and events long-past. And all can be used as fodder for lively class discussion, for making the subjects we're teaching come alive.

We might take pride in saying we never watch television, but we shouldn't be so quick to put it down—especially as it pertains to teaching. Television is one thing students have in common, and I think it was Winston Churchhill who said, "The only thing worse than democracy is any other form of government." I think the same can be said for television: "The only thing worse than television is no television." Sure, theres a lot on that's not worth watching, but theres also a lot that is. And to ignore it's influence is to ignore an excellent, if flawed, teaching tool.

Sample "3" Essay

I sometimes wish TV had never been invented. Especially for the younger generation, who get much of their information about the world in a distorted fashion from "the box." Of course it is entertaining after a hard day, but at the end what have you gained?

And the news gets distorted. We get our news from "a reliabel source" but who is that? Some gossip columnist in Washington or New York that has nothing to do with our real life. We get to see how rotten our politicions are and maybe thats a good thing because earlier in history they could cover it up. We get to

watch them on TV and judge for ourself instead of taking someone else's word for it. So television can be a good thing if watched in moderation.

Another way TV corrups society is through advertizing. It tells us to buy, buy, buy. It gives us super models and sport's figures to tell you what to buy and where. It gives you movie stars advertizing even in a TV movie away from comercials, by holding a can of Coke or other product. All of which subliminaly tells you to buy Coke. They say they even have messages flashed on the screen so on the commercial you will get up and go to the kitchen. I find myself bringing home products I never even use. The worse thing is the shows in which dificult life situatsions get solved in a half hour. You could never do it in real life but on TV it is easy. It gives us a erronous view of the world.

I think we should try to do away with it in our homes even if it is hard. After all, its your baby-sitter and advise-giver, and even your friend if you are lonely. But give it a week to be away from it and then watch intermitently. You're life will be better for it.

Sample "1" Essay

TV can be good or bad depending on how you look at it. It can be all you do if you are not careful. It can take you away from your kids if you use it as a baby sitter or when you come home from work that is all you do. Also you will never get the real story. You will never know if they are telling the truth or trying a snow job to sell you something.

I grew up with television like most peopel. It is a good thing if you try to learn from it. It probably will help in a class room discussion if the children all watch the same show. In grade school where I went we had current events and television had it's place.

One example is the news. We know if we are going to war the minute the president makes his decission. We can watch it all happening. We can know if there is a scandel in Washington. And the latest medical facts are on TV. So TV can be good in that aspect.

It can be bad to. For example the shows for teen agers. When I was a teen ager I liked them, all the music and the dancing. But now it is diferent. Drugs are spread through MTV because of the musicions who you can tell do them. And they are models for our kids.

But in some aspects TV is good and in some it is bad. I think spending time away from it will make you feel better. all the news is bad news. But you can get an education too if you just watch public TV. It is good in some aspects and bad in some.

479.

Sample "6" Essay
Life is full of problems, but the method we use to approach those problems often determines whether we're happy or miserable. Bob Maynard says, "Problems are opportunities in disguise." If we approach problems with Maynard's attitude, we can see that problems are really opportunities to learn about others and ourselves. They enable us to live happier and more fulfilling lives.

Maynard's quote applies to all kinds of problems. To share a personal story, I faced a problem just last week when our family's kitchen sink developed a serious leak. Water puddled all over our new kitchen floor, and to make matters worse, our landlord was out of town for the week. Since my family is large, we couldn't afford to wait for the landlord's return nor could we afford an expensive plumbing bill. Taking charge, I decided to learn how to fix it myself. The best place to start was at my local library. There, I found a great fix-it-yourself book, and in just a few hours, I had figured out the cause of the leak. Not only did I repair the leak, but I know now that I can rely on my own abilities to solve other everyday problems.

I think it's important to remember that no matter how big a problem is; it's still an opportunity. Whatever kind of situation we face, problems give us the chance to learn and grow, both physically and mentally. Problems challenge us and give us the chance to do things we've never done before, to learn things we never knew before. They teach us what we're capable of doing, and often they give us the chance to surprise ourselves.

Sample "4" Essay
Just the word "problem" can send some of us into a panic. But problems can be good things, too. Problems are situations that make us think and force us to be creative and resourceful. They can also teach us things we didn't know before.

For example, I had a problem in school a few years ago when I couldn't understand my math class. I started failing my quizzes and homework assignments. I wasn't sure what to do, so finally I went to the teacher and asked for help. She said she would arrange for me to be tutored by another student who was her best student. In return, though, I'd have to help that student around school. I wasn't sure what she meant by that until I met my tutor. She was handicapped.

My job was to help her carry her books from class to class. I'd never even spoken to someone in a wheelchair before and I was a little scared. But she turned out to be the nicest person I've ever spent time with. She helped me understand everything I need to know for math class and she taught me a lot about what it's like to be handicapped. I learned to appreciate everything that I have, and I also know that people with disabilities are special not because of what they can't do, but because of who they are.

So you see that wonderful things can come out of problems. You just have to remember to look for the positive things and not focus on the negative.

Sample "3" Essay

The word "problem" is a negative word but its just an opportunity as Mr. Bob Maynard has said. It can be teaching tool besides.

For example, I had a problem with my son last year when he wanted a bigger allowance. I said no and he had to earn it. He mowed the lawn and in the fall he raked leaves. In the winter he shovelled the walk. After that he apreciated it more.

Its not the problem but the sollution that matters. My son learning the value of work and earning money. (It taught me the value of money to when I had to give him a bigger allowance!) After that he could get what he wanted at Toys Are Us and not have to beg. Which was better for me too. Sometimes we forget that both children and there parents can learn a lot from problems and we can teach our children the value of over-coming trouble. Which is as important as keeping them out of trouble. As well we can teach them the value of money. That is one aspect of a problem that we manytimes forget.

So problems are a good teaching tool as well as a good way to let you're children learn, to look at the silver lining behind every cloud.

Sample "1" Essay

I agree with the quote that problems are opportunities in disguise. Sometimes problems are opportunities, too.

I have a lot of problems like anyone else does. Sometimes there very difficult and I don't no how to handle them. When I have a really big problem, I sometimes ask my parents or freinds for advise. Sometimes they help, sometimes they don't, then I have to figure out how to handle it myself.

One time I had a big problem. Where someone stole my wallet and I had to get to a job interview. But I had no money and no ID. This happen in school. So I went to the principles office and reported it. He called the man I was supposed to interview with. Who rescheduled the intervew for me. So I still had the opportunity to interview and I'm proud to say I got the job. In fact I'm still working there!

Problems can be opportunities if you just look at them that way. Instead of the other way around.

SET 46 (Page 113)

480.

Sample "6" Essay

Courage and cowardice seem like absolutes. We are often quick to label other people, or ourselves, as either "brave" or "timid," "courageous" or "cowardly." However, one bright afternoon on a river deep in the wilds of the Ozark mountains, I learned that these qualities are as changeable as mercury.

During a cross-country drive, my friend Nina and I decided to stop at a campsite in Missouri and spend the afternoon on a boat trip down Big Piney River, 14 miles through the wilderness. We rented a canoe and paddled happily off. Things were fine for the first seven or eight miles. We gazed at the overhanging bluffs, commented on the dogwoods in bloom, and marveled at the clarity of the water. Then, in approaching Devil's Elbow, a bend in the river, the current suddenly swept us in toward the bank, under the low-hanging branches of a weeping willow. The canoe tipped over, and I was pulled under. My foot caught for just a few seconds on the willow's submerged roots, and just as I surfaced, I saw the canoe sweeping out, upright again, but empty. Nina was frantically swimming after it.

Standing by cravenly, I knew I should help, but I was petrified. I let my friend brave the treacherous rapids and haul the canoe back onto the gravel bar by herself. But then came the scream, and Nina dashed back into the water. In the bottom of the canoe, a black and brown, checkerboard-patterned copperhead snake lay coiled. I don't know exactly why, but the inborn terror of snakes is something that has passed me by completely. I actually find them rather charming in a scaly sort of way, but Nina was still screaming. In a calm way that must have seemed smug, I said, "We're in its home, it's not in ours." And gently, I prodded it with the oar until it reared up, slithered over the side of the canoe, and raced away.

Later that night, in our cozy, safe motel room, we agreed that we each had cold chills thinking about what might have happened. Still, I learned something important from the ordeal. I know that, had we encountered only the rapids, I might have come away ashamed, labeling myself a coward, and had we encountered only the snake, Nina might have done the same. I also know that neither of us will ever again be quite so apt to brand another person as lacking courage. Because we will always know that, just around the corner, may be the snake or the bend in the river or the figure in the shadows or something else as yet unanticipated, that will cause our own blood to freeze.

Sample "4" Essay

Courage can be shown in many ways and by many kinds of people. One does not have to be rich, or educated, or even an adult to show true courage.

For example, a very heartbreaking thing happened in our family. It turned out all right but at the time it almost made us lose our faith. However, it also taught us a lesson regarding courage. In spite of his father's and my repeated warnings, my son Matt went ice-fishing with some friends and fell through the ice into the frigid water beneath. He is prone to do things that are dangerous no matter how many times he's told. Fortunately there were grown-ups near and they were able to throw him a life line and pull him to safety. However, when they got him onto shore they discovered he was unconscious. There were vital signs

but they were weak, the paramedics pronounced him in grave danger.

He is his little sisters (Nans) hero. He is 16 and she is 13, just at the age where she admires everything he does. When they took him to the hospital she insisted on going that night to see him, and she insisted on staying with me there. My husband thought we should insist she go home, but it was Christmas vacation for her so there was no real reason. So we talked it over and she stayed. She stayed every night for the whole week just to be by Matt's side. And when he woke up she was there. Her smiling face the was first thing he saw.

In spite of the fact she was just a child and it was frightning for her to be there beside her brother she loves so much, and had to wonder, every day if he would die, she stayed. So courage has many faces.

Sample "3" Essay

Courage is not something we are born with. It is something that we have to learn.

For example when your children are growing up you should teach them courage. Teach them to face lifes challanges and not to show there fear. For instance my father. Some people would say he was harsh, but back then I didnt think of it that way. One time he took me camping and I had a tent of my own. I wanted to crawl in with him but he said there was nothing to be afraid of. And I went to sleep sooner than I would have expect. He taught me not to be afraid.

There are many reasons for courage. In a war a solder has to be couragous and a mother has to be no less couragous if she is rasing a child alone and has to make a living. So, in me it is totally alright to be afraid as long as you face your fear. I have been greatful to him ever since that night.

Sometimes parents know what is best for there kids even if at the time it seems like a harsh thing. I learned not to show my fear that night, which is an important point to courage. In everyday life it is important to learn how to be strong. If we dont learn from our parents, like I did from my father, then we have to learn it after we grow up. But it is better to learn it, as a child. I have never been as afriad as I was that night, and I learned a valuble lesson from it.

Sample "1" Essay
Courage is important in a battle and also ordinary life. In a war if your buddy depends on you and you let him down he might die. Courage is also important in daly life. If you have sicknes in the famly or if you enconter a mugger on the street you will need all the courage you can get. There are many dangers in life that only courage will see you through.

Once, my apartment was burglerised and they stole a TV and micro-wave. I didnt have very much. They took some money to. I felt afraid when I walked in and saw things moved or gone. But I call the police and waited for them inside my apartment which was brave and also some might say stupid! But the police came and took my statement and also later caught the guy. Another time my girlfreind and I were in my apartment and we looked out the window and there was somebody suspisious out in front. It turned out to be a false alarm but she was scard and she said because I was calm it made her feel better. So courage was important to me, in my relatinship with my girlfeind.

So courage is importand not only in war but also in life.

481.

Sample "6" Essay
Writing, at least the kind of basic composition needed to be successful in school, can be taught. The most important factor in teaching a basic composition class, which usually has students who have been less than successful writers in the past, is a simple one. The student should be asked to write about something inter-esting in a context with a purpose beyond "English class." In other words, the student should *want* to learn to write. For students who have fallen behind for one reason or another, it's difficult to see a writing class as anything but an exercise in plummeting self-esteem. Many students believe that writing well is a mystery only those "with talent" can understand, and that "English class" is just something to endure. The first thing to teach students is that writing has a purpose that pertains to their lives. The teacher must appeal to emotion as well as to intellect.

I believe the best approach is to ask students to keep a journal in two parts. In one part, grammar and style shouldn't matter, the way they have to matter in the formal assignments that come later in the course. In this part of the journal, the students should be asked to keep track of things they encounter during the day that interest them or cause them to be happy, sad, angry, or afraid. In the second part of the journal they should keep track of subjects that make them sit up and take notice. These can include things that happen in class or ideas that come to them when reading an assignment for class. These journal notes should whet the intellect and excite curiosity.

For teaching grammar, the teacher can present exercises in the context of a one-page essay or story because it gives writing a context. Too often in the early grades, students complete dry drill and skill exercises that take the fun out of writing. Diagramming sentences, identifying nouns and verbs, or labeling adjectives seems far removed from the skill of writing. Appeal to emotion, intellect, and curiosity will really succeed in engaging the whole student and awakening the urge to write.

Sample "4" Essay
I believe writing can be taught if we work hard enough at it as teachers. The important thing is to teach students that it can be enjoyable. Years of fearing writing

lie behind a lot of students, and it's one of the biggest stumbling blocks. But it can be gotten over.

Having them break up into small groups is one way to teach writing to reluctant or ill-prepared students. Have the students discuss a topic they are all interested in—say a recent TV show or an event coming up at school, then plan a paper and come back and discuss the idea with the whole class. Your next step can be to have them actually write the paper, then get into their small groups again and criticize what theyve done.

Another way for students who don't like the small groups is one on one conferences. But dont just talk about grammar or sentence structure or paragraphing, talk about the content of his paper. I did a summer internship teaching in an innter city school, and I rememmber one young man. He hated small groups so we talked privately. He had written a paper on going to a city-sponsored camping trip and seeing white-tailed deer, which was his first time. He was excited about it, and I suggested he write a paper about his experience. He did and, except for some trouble with grammar, it was an A paper, full of active verbs and telling detail!

Finally, try to get your students to read. If you have to, drag them to the community library yourself. Not only will it help their writing, it will help them in life. Only by getting them interested in the written word and by helping them to see that it matters in their everyday lives can you really reach them and set them on the path of good writing.

Yes. Writing can be taught if you are willing to take the time and do the hard work and maybe give a few extra hours. No student is hopeless. And writing is so important in today's world that its worth the extra effort.

Sample "3" Essay

I dont think writing can be taught neccesarily, although if the students are half-way motivated anything's possible. The first thing is get them interested in the subject and give them alot of writing to do in class. They may not do it if it is all outside class as many poorly prepared students hate homework. I know I did as a kid!

Writing does not come natural for most people especially in the poorer school districs. Unless they are lucky enough to have parents who read to them. That is another aspect of teaching how to write. Assign alot of reading. If you don't read you can't write, and that is lacking in alot of students backgrounds. If your students wont' read books tell them to read comic books if nothing else. Anything to get them to read.

The second thing is to have the student come in for a conference once a week. That is one way to see what is going on with them in school and at home. A lot of kids in the poorer schools have conflict at home and that is why they fail. So give them alot of praise because thats what they need.

Finaly don't give up. It can be done. Many people born into poverty go on to do great things. You can help and you never know who you will inspire and who will remember you as the best teacher they ever had.

Sample "1" Essay

You will be able to tell I am one of the peopel that never learned to write well. I wish I had but my personal experience as a struggleing writer will inspire my students, thats the most I can hope for. Writing can be taught, but you have to be ready to inspire the student. Give them assignments on subjets they like and keep after them to read. Take them to the public libary if they havnt been and introduce them to books.

If you cant write people will call you dumb or stupid which hurts you're self-estem. I know from experience.

The next thing is have them come in and talk to you. You never know what is going on in there lifes that is keeping them from studying and doing there best. Maybe they have a mom that works all the time or a dad who has left the home. Be sure to teach the whole person. Also have them write about what is going on in there lives, not a dry subject like the drinking age. Have the student write about there personal experience and it will come out better. Writing can be taught if the student is motivated. So hang in there.

These sample essays show you how the scoring guide works. There are no sample essays for the rest of the topics in Section 6. Simply use the scoring rubric on pages 150–151 to evaluate your essays. Remember, it's better to have someone else read your essay than to try to evaluate it yourself.

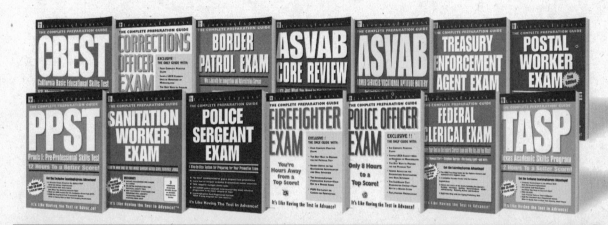